T0345153

Automated Software
Testing with Cypress

Automated Software Testing with Cypress

Narayanan Palani

CRC Press
Taylor & Francis Group
Boca Raton London New York

CRC Press is an imprint of the
Taylor & Francis Group, an **informa** business

AN AUERBACH BOOK

first edition published 2021
by CRC Press
6000 Broken Sound Parkway NW, Suite 300, Boca Raton, FL 33487-2742

and by CRC Press
2 Park Square, Milton Park, Abingdon, Oxon, OX14 4RN

Library of Congress Cataloging-in-Publication Data
A catalog record has been requested for this book.

ISBN: 978-0-367-75968-1 (hbk)
ISBN: 978-0-367-69954-3 (pbk)
ISBN: 978-1-003-14511-0 (ebk)

Typeset in Garamond
by KnowledgeWorks Global Ltd.

To my teacher
Mrs. Tamil Selvi Viswanathan

Contents

About the Author

Narayanan Palani is a quality engineering chapter lead of major financial institution in United Kingdom. He specializes in automation, accessibility, performance and security testing. Narayanan has certifications from Microsoft, Scaled Agile, DevOps Institute, International Software Testing Qualifications Board, International Software Quality Institute, with an MS in Software Engineering and Executive MBA. His online courses are subscribed by at least 35000+ students across 158+ countries worldwide. Narayanan is the author of the book series 'Software Automation Testing Secrets Revealed' and receiver of 'Best Test Manager of the Year' award from European Software Testing Awards, Year 2019.

Introduction

As an automation specialist, I have been focussing on implementing test automation solutions on three stages, i.e., Unit Integration Testing (UIT), System Integration Testing (SIT) and Regression Testing.

Since 2014, Selenium has been the best tool to implement for SIT and regression phases and I found it useful to choose JavaScript version (WebdriverIO) for the front-end applications, which are built around nodejs JavaScript. But, UIT had been a challenge since there was no tool that could help in XHR programming and UI validations in an efficient way until Cypress.io arrived. Cypress.io started releasing earlier versions in the year 2015, but became extremely popular from the year 2018 with version 2.0.0 onwards. I have been exploring Cypress scripts since then and it gives a lot of excitement and opportunity to start implementing Cypress part of 'shift left testing', which is a dream come true moment for me. Shift left is a jargon used in the majority of testing projects, but it has not been possible 100% to implement it due to the unavailability of tool and knowledge about the possibilities of getting testing done early in the life cycle. Shift left is a key test strategy to make the teams reduce focussing on defect identifications and start developing practices on defect prevention methodology. When Cypress.io scripts were developed initially, I found them extremely useful for both front-end developers and quality engineers, as they can work together to find defects soon after the web components are built and tested immediately with Cypress.io Test Driven Development (TDD) scripts! Thus, defects get fixed immediately during the development stage itself, which avoids the need to worry about the same defect in later stages, since Cypress tests keep verifying those components in later stages, and thus, defect fixing is extremely cheaper as compared to finding those defects in Selenium tests later on as a part of SIT and regression, which is a bit expensive to get the defects fixed and test them as part of retesting. I have covered various selenium automation frameworks part of 'Software Automation Testing Secrets Revealed- Book Series Part1,2 and 3: advanced selenium web accessibility testing

As the next step, I have built Behaviour Driven Development (BDD)-based Gherkin scrits around Cypress with the help of Cypress Cucumber preprocessor, which make a lucrative improvement in test scenario coverage, since BDD-based user stories (requirements) have started getting implemented as Cypress Gherkin scripts in order to run the unit integration tests.

This book has been written to fulfil both BDD and TDD needs of testing teams*. Hence, there are two distinct open source repositories provided in Github for you to download and start running Cypress tests in no time! In addition to Github repositories, video tutorials are available for readers to refer at popular websites such as https://engineers-hub.teachable.com/

Behaviour Driven Development Using Cypress

Cypress BDD Repository is named as 'cypress test techniques' and it can be downloaded from https://github.com/narayananpalani/cypress-test-techniques.

---

* **Note**
  This book should not be construed as documentation for Cypress or any tools described. At the time of this writing, Cypress v4.0 has been used as reference. Please refer https://www.cypress.io/ for later version and features

Installation: Perform following commands in a new terminal:

```
npm install
npm link
npm link cypress-cucumber-preprocessor
npm install through
```

Application: There is a sample demo application (online application) used for Cypress tests in order to show command examples on each test written in the BDD format.

Launch Cypress Tests: Open another terminal and enter 'npx cypress open' to launch Cypress tests.

Test Driven Development Using Cypress

Cypress TDD Repository is named as 'cypress api test techniques' and it can be downloaded from https://github.com/narayananpalani/cypress-api-test-techniques.

Installation: Open a command line terminal and enter 'npm i cypress --save-dev'.

Launch Web Application: Open a command line terminal (new terminal dedicated to application) and enter 'npx serve' to launch the sample application, which is used for Cypress tests.

Launch Cypress Tests: Open another terminal and enter 'npm run e2e' to launch Cypress tests.

Locators

Similar to 'Descriptive Programming' of Unified Functional Testing (formerly QTP), Cypress scripting requires the basic knowledge of object capturing techniques using CSS Selectors and XPath. This section will explain the type of CSS, XPath elements and usage guidelines.

During my earlier days with Selenium scripting, most of the tests become non-scalable complex test framework within few years of time and difficult to fix object issues as a surprise! When I investigated during the test failure every time, it would go to the DOM elements and tell me that the object properties of the application have been changed or added with additional suffix or prefix on the existing properties I have used. Most engineers prefer to use a unique locator such as data-selector or qa-selector or ID of the object (at least) instead of using CSS or name or class of the object properties.

The most unique XPath is the most reliable!

If the following types are still failing, I would suggest you to ask developers to add a new object (tag) with description what you want (may be you can ask for qa-selector field like ID)!

Types:

- ■ ID (Unique locator)
- ■ Class
- ■ Name
- ■ Value
- ■ Text (Link text, partial link text)
- ■ XPath (Relative X path)
- ■ CSS (Fastest locator)
- ■ DOM

If none of the above works for you at times, use qa-selector (a dedicated locator agreed with developers to write for every object written by dev team to include additional property such as qa-selector for the need of running automated tests).

Maintaining object properties of the Application Under Test (AUT) is one of the most complex areas during the script maintenance and migration of application across infrastructure movements. HTML properties such as name, id, title, CSS and XPath can be added to automation framework in order to perform tests on such objects. ID and XPath are some of the most famous object reference techniques across various test automation tools. Having unique object locator such as 'qa-selector' will help maintaining the test pack healthy. But, the challenge is that developers are to follow this routine to add qa-selector as a property for every object they add to the web page such as text box, buttons, links, etc. If there are newly joined developers in team, it will be difficult to assume that they know to add such unique selectors to favour testers.

Cypress generally accepts CSS selectors as object property in order to perform tests. If you are using Google Chrome, it is very easy to record scripts for Cypress using 'Cypress Recorder', an extension made for Google Chrome in which auto-generated Cypress scripts can be copied and used in automation frameworks.

Install Cypress Recorder from https://chrome.google.com/webstore/detail/cypress-recorder/glcapdcacdfkokcmicllhcjigeodacab.

XPath of object properties can be used across Cypress scripts if cypress-xpath is installed as part of npm installation; I have used the version 1.3.0, and also, used varieties of XPaths across links, text boxes and other html properties.

If you are not using this tool within your Cypress scripts, please install it by

```
npm install cypress-xpath
```

Note for the path `cypress/support/index.js`: Make sure to include the configuration at the project path within the automation framework.

```
require('cypress-xpath')
```

Locating by XPath

In XML documents, XPath is the language used to locate nodes, which is the same name used for automation tests to locate the object XPath. It can be used to either locate the object element in absolute terms (but not suggested), or relative to an element that does have an id or name attribute within XML file.

Absolute XPaths contain the exact location of all elements from the root (html) and as a result, are likely to fail during execution with only the slightest adjustment to the web application.

Find the item with id or name or any nearby object property, which is less likely to change in the near future and update the script with "//" like the example below:

Example:

```
id="searchbox_016909259827549404702:hzru01fldsm"
title="seleniumhq.org Selenium Search"
action="http://www.google.com/cse">
  <div>
    <label title="Search SeleniumHQ.org's sites for
selenium content" for="q"></label>
    <input type="hidden" value="005991058577830013072:
2lr_j6t3fko" name="cx"></input>
    <input type="hidden" value="FORID:"
name="cof"></input>
    <input id="q" type="text" size="30"
accesskey="s" name="q"></input>
    <input id="submit" type="submit"
value="Go"></input>
  </div>
</form
```

In the list of properties available in html format, id="q" is the object id of the search box, which is important for testing. Get this q to update the script as below:

```
cy.xpath('//input[@id="q"]')
```

Locating by CSS

Rendering of html and XML documents are described in cascading style sheets known as CSS.

How a Selenium beginner understands CSS locator and how to capture such object property is explained in the below example:

Launch seleniumhq.org web page in Firefox:

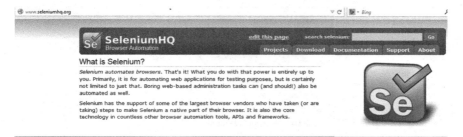

Web page of seleniumhq

Launch Selenium IDE on the other side and keep it open:

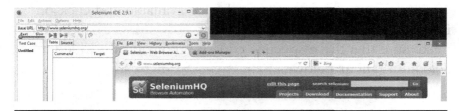

Selenium IDE along with seleniumhq web page

Selenium IDE is opened just to get more command options when the object is right clicked!

Now, right click on the Go button on top right corner:

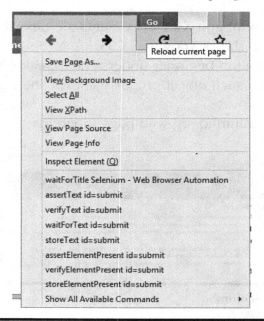

Selenium IDE options

Choose any command from the list available and click on it (for example: choose `verifyText id=submit`) and then make sure that the respective code is automatically added to Selenium IDE as below:

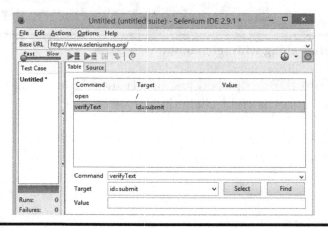

Selenium IDE version 2.9.1

Now, click on the dropdown in Target section and there must be a list of XPath options available for the same object, which can be chosen alternatively:

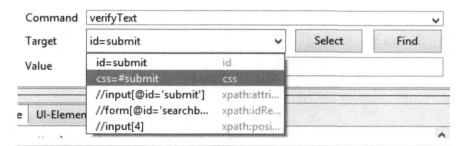

CSS selector within Target field of Selenium IDE

CSS of the Go button is #submit, which is taken from this place and it can be verified from Inspect Element:

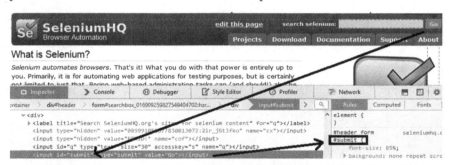

Inspect Element section to check the object properties on seleniumhq web page

This CSS selector can be used in Cypress scripts as below:

```
cy.get('#submit')
```

Chapter 1

Visual Regression

Traditionally, organisations perform functional testing along with non-functional testing such as performance and security/vulnerability testing in order to release their code. But earlier, in application life cycle, there was no solution to the User Interface (UI) problems such as alignment changes and minor object relocation, which look bad when launching the web pages, but never be possible to notice all of them during the functional test runs. If a text box appears on the left-hand side of a page (as per the requirement) and even if it is re-aligned to the bottom right-hand side of the page, the automated tests would still pass since the object (in this case, text box) is found in this scenario. But, as per the requirement, it was difficult in the past to verify the text box exactly at a particular height and width and manual testing was the only solution to get this verification done until visual testing has been introduced.

Visual testing is nothing but the pixel by pixel comparison of the images of the test pages with the pre-saved screenshots of those pages to see how they look like when the latest code has been deployed. Since there are target pages getting saved historically, it is easy to compare them in automated code.

What if you haven't done your visual testing yet and hence, no records of images have been saved for comparison?

Do not worry—during your first run of the tests, it will save the target screenshots and you can verify them before running your next test on the re-deployed next version of the code.

Benefits of Visual Testing with Cypress

As a Software Development Engineer in Test (SDeT), I have been using visual tests within the selenium framework and finding issues to get them fixed at UI level. But, performing visual tests at right side of the test cycle is really late since the code has already been gone through unit testing, system testing and progressing towards regression testing. That's true!

A majority of the projects use selenium kind of automation tools at the right-hand side of the project to automate only when the QA has some time to automate. The major disadvantage of this approach is the expense occurred to fix every defect of the application since it has already crossed several stages of the application development and testing.

When visual testing is performed in Cypress, it provides the right solution to test visuals right after the page has been built. It means the application has not even gone through unit testing yet!

At this stage, finding a defect makes less expense compared to finding the same defect after System Integration Testing (SIT) or during regression test phase.

Since Cypress is used at application development level to make changes to UI code and rerun tests to see the user behaviour, running visual testing helps in fixing the alignment issues, colour issues and height-weight related issues during application development itself. Hence, it is an extreme shift level model of performing UI visual testing!

Basics

Usually, visual regression tests produce three types of snapshots:

- Base files: When the tests were run in the past, the first screenshot of the page or object during the successful test was stored in the base file location as the first snapshot to be used for any visual comparison. In Cypress, this file gets stored at the following path:
  `\cypress\snapshots\features`
- Screenshots: Every time the test runs successfully at the following path:
  `\cypress\snapshots\features`
- Differences: Any differences between the base file (of first successful run) and the latest screenshot evidence is kept under the following path:
  `\cypress\snapshots\features\`*`<name>`*`.`
  `feature\ __ diff _ output __`

Note: `.feature` file name varies based on the type and name of the feature file used for visual testing.

Sample Visual Test Defect using Cypress

Visual test
- Check visual test failed
  - ○ TEST
  - **LOG** Given I open homepage
  - **VISIT/**
  - **LOG** And I capture snapshot and compare "loginpage"
  - **TASK** Matching image snapshot, Object{3}
  - **SCREENSHOT** loginpage
  - **TASK** Recording snapshot result
  - **THEN** function(){}

Error
Image was 0.6824884792626728% different from saved snapshot with 5924 different pixels. See diff for

```
details: E:\Udemy\github\cypress\cypress-test-
techniques\cypress\snapshots\features\
loginVisualTest.feature_diff_output_\loginpage.
diff.png
View stack trace
Error: Image was 0.6824884792626728% different from
saved snapshot with 5924 different pixels. See diff
for details: E:\Udemy\github\cypress\cypress-test-
techniques\cypress\snapshots\features\
loginVisualTest.feature\__diff_output__\loginpage.
diff.png at Context.<anonymous> (https://
opensource-demo.orangehrmlive.com/__cypress/
tests?p=cypress\integration\features\
loginVisualTest.feature-406:10316:17) From previous
event: at Context.thenFn (https://opensource-demo.
orangehrmlive.com/__cypress/runner/cypress_runner.
js:132255:23)
```

Let us understand on how to configure such simple
but powerful visual regression tests using Cypress.
io! I am using two tools for Cypress visual regression at
`package.json`:

```
"cypress-visual-regression": "1.0.4",
"cypress-image-snapshot": "3.1.1",
```

Since both these tools are compatible with Cypress 4.4.1, I
have installed both of them with the commands below:

Installation from command line or Github or terminal using
the commands:

```
npm install cypress-visual-regression -g
npm install cypress-image-snapshot -g
```

The reason we need two different tools for visual regression
is pretty simple. Cypress-image-snapshot provides us the
snapshots from each tests being run as part of visual
regression, and cypress-visual-regression helps in finding
any mismatches between the base file and the current test's

screenshot to provide differences in the folder __diff_output__ as a visual test result!

Once both these tools are installed along with Cypress, update commands javascript file at \cypress\support\ commands.js with the commands below:

```
const compareSnapshotCommand = require('cypress-
visual-regression/dist/command')
import {addMatchImageSnapshotCommand}  from
'cypress-image-snapshot/command'
import 'cypress-file-upload';


compareSnapshotCommand()
addMatchImageSnapshotCommand({
  failureThreshold: 0.00,
  failureThresholdType: 'percent',
  customDiffConfig: {threshold: 0.0},
  capture: 'fullPage',
  timeout: '60000',
})
```

Once commands.js has been updated, next is to update index javascript file in plugins folder at the following path \cypress\plugins\index.js for the configurations of snapshot comparisons. Make sure to add both getCompareSnapshotsPlugin and addMatchImageSnapshotPlugin within modules.export along with cucumber preprocessor if you are running cucumber tests:

```
const getCompareSnapshotsPlugin =
require('cypress-visual-regression/dist/plugin')
const {
  addMatchImageSnapshotPlugin,
} = require('cypress-image-snapshot/plugin')

module.exports = (on, config) => {
  on('file:preprocessor', cucumber())
```

```
getCompareSnapshotsPlugin(on)
addMatchImageSnapshotPlugin(on, config)

}
```

Optionally, scripts can be added into `package.json` to be used as a simplified command for visual tests such as below:

```
"scripts": {
  "test:visual-base": "cypress run -b chrome
--env updateSnapshots=true -spec cypress/
integration/features/*VisualTest.feature",
  "test:visual-actual": "cypress run -b chrome
--env failOnSnapshotDiff=false --reporter
cypress-image-snapshot/reporter --spec cypress/
integration/features/*VisualTest.feature"
},
```

Once configuration is done, writing a sample visual test feature file looks like this:

```
Feature: First visual test

  Scenario: check My website through visual test
    Given I open the homepage
    And I capture snapshot and compare
"loginpage"
    When I SignIn as user
    Then the username should be displayed
    And I capture snapshot and compare
"homepage"
```

As you know now that the last line (marked bold) is the visual testing part of it.

I have written a step definition in `shared.js` (path: \cypress\support\step _ definitions\Shared.js) file to link this feature file line as below:

```
then('I capture snapshot and compare {string}',
(string) => {
```

```
   cy.matchImageSnapshot(string);
});
```

Let us understand how this visual test is overall using the configuration which is very critical here.

Match Image Snapshot of Cypress Command

It takes the string from feature file to process the snapshot comparison by using the functions stated in index:
  getCompareSnapshotsPlugin and
addMatchImageSnapshotPlugin
  All looks great but why it is not popular these days?
The answer is false positive! Every tool is really good only when we have a good maintenance and manage custom configurations according to the project's needs from time to time.
  Command.js has got a configuration to update the threshold level, which needs to be revised every time when the project or application goes through major releases or changes here:

```
addMatchImageSnapshotCommand({
   failureThreshold: 0.00,
   failureThresholdType: 'percent',
   customDiffConfig:  {threshold: 0.0},
   capture: 'fullPage',
   timeout: '60000',
})
```

Having failureThreshold of 0.00 will simply give unwanted test failures part of visual regression according to my two years' experience with visual tests (across WebdriverIO, Cypress, BackstopJS and few other tools).

Visual Tests in Agile Test Life Cycle

It is easy to adapt a visual test tool such as BackstopJS or Cypress within the automation test framework, but it is not that useful if used at the later stages of the project when few or less Graphical User Interface (GUI) defects are expected to get leaked. So, it is highly advisable to implement visual tests just in line with the development of GUI code. While a front-end engineer is building a web page or a small web component, testers should build visual tests and run the GUI comparison tests to spot any visual issue as a general practice. This will help in running visual regression when the application grows old, and also, help in finding bugs when any small defect fixes or small releases make some dramatic html alignment issues within the web elements. Generally, functional defects of cases such as object missing or the disabled field exposed through visual test result if they run early in the life cycle.

Easy Implementation at High Level

The implementation part takes just four steps:

1. Install cypress-image-snapshot
2. Update Commands.js
3. Write Behaviour Driven Development (BDD) image comparison
4. Write step definition to call matchImageSnapshot

Two Types of Key Screenshots

1. Snapshot taken in earlier cycle which is saved in snapshots folder (which is same as Base)
2. Difference found during visual testing which is stored in__*diff_output*__ folder

Testing the web application needs some basic knowledge about how these visual tests work in real time when using along with BDD-based Cypress Frameworks.

When running the visual regression tests, the difference between the actual and the expected snapshots loads in the feature file at the following paths:

Snapshots: \cypress\snapshots\features*.feature\
Differences: \cypress\snapshots\features*.
   feature__diff_output__

If you are running complete specifications, test snapshots get saved at location:

Snapshot: \cypress\snapshots\All Specs\
Differences: \cypress\snapshots\All Specs__diff_output__

False Results during Visual Testing

When tests are performed in test environments using test data across organisations, data vary from one to the other; so, the UI displays custom details of respective test data on the screen.

Hence, visual testing captures the complete page, including those data elements on the UI level, and fails when there are data changes from the previous runs to the current run. So, it is not appropriate for engineers to raise defects for a false negative result of visual tests failing for no valid reason.

Even if there is a small change in the UI colours, it is possible to fail the tests.

Solution:
Adjust the threshold levels here in `commands.js` file:

```
addMatchImageSnapshotCommand({
   failureThreshold: 0.05,
```

```
    failureThresholdType: 'percent',
    customDiffConfig: {threshold: 0.1},
    capture: 'fullPage',
    timeout: '60000',
})
```

If you want to take screenshot comparisons during your compatibility tests across tablet, mobile devices mode, it is preferred to change the capture mode to viewport:

```
addMatchImageSnapshotCommand({
  failureThreshold: 0.05,
  failureThresholdType: 'percent',
  customDiffConfig: { threshold: 0.1 },
  capture: 'viewport',
  timeout: '60000',
})
```

Compatibility of Visual Testing with the Right Version of Cypress

Cypress-image-snapshot@>2.0.0 needs to be used for any Cypress version above 3.0.2.

Need custom visual testing for selected objects

When complex UI has been built in dynamic loading web pages using ReactJS or other JS components, it may not be relevant to take the complete page screenshot to compare a part of visual testing since it is irrelevant if the page is just designed as single page website to display to get it expanded when scrolling down to the respective sections.

Let us take an example of a password text field and verify this particular field for the difference in look and feel to get it compared with the available snapshots.

Solution:

Use specific objects to compare with the snapshots to find the differences visually. Example:

```
cy.get('#txtPassword').matchImageSnapshot();
```

How to Implement the Visual Testing When a Huge Number of Pages are Getting Built?

In large organisations, thousands of web pages are getting built every hour to produce their delivery needs and get them tested manually or through automation. When considering visual testing for those types of huge number of pages in one go, the best option in visual testing is to use it as `cy.visit` level.

It means that matchImageSnapshot needs to be called when launching every new page for testing using Cypress:

```
describe('Login', () => {
  it('should be publicly accessible', () => {
    cy.visit('/home');
    cy.matchImageSnapshot();
  });
});
```

Snapshot name will be the test title in the example above as per the Github instructions at https://github.com/palmerhq/cypress-image-snapshot.

Chapter 2

Web Accessibility Testing

Testing accessibility against Web Content Accessibility Guidelines (WCAG) and/or Section 508 rules needs three types of testing:

1. Accessibility audit (when the web component getting developed)
2. Accessibility tests (using screen readers, magnifiers and other equipment manually)
3. Accessibility automated regression tests (writing regression tests with html properties, which are incorporated to provide better accessibility such as aria-label, title etc.)

Accessibility Audit using Axe and Cypress.io

Thanks to Deque Corporation for providing axe as an extension to google chrome and also a Node Package Manager (npm) package to integrate in automated tests. To give a little background on the accessibility audit, pa11y is the very first tool which has been used in javascript-based automated frameworks to scan the websites to provide accessibility violations.

```
Installation: npm install -g pally
```

Once installed, go to terminal (of Webstorm IDE or Visual Studio IDE) and type:

pally https://www.github.com

Pally tool provides the complete audit results of a particular page, but it will not help if a particular page has to be audited/scanned after performing login or any actions to move away from this page in order to land on page 2 or 3 to get it scanned. Pally-ci is another option which can be integrated to continuous integration, but it was not that popular until axe came into picture and helped us in finding accessibility violations during the application development.

This tool can be installed as an extension to Google Chrome:

https://chrome.google.com/webstore/detail/
axe-web-accessibility-tes/lhdoppojpmngadmnindnejefpokejbdd

The latest version of axe available as axe-coconut is an exploratory version:

https://chrome.google.com/webstore/detail/axe-coconut-
web-accessibi/iobddmbdndbbbfjopjdgadphaoihpojp?hl
=en

The main challenge with the chrome extension is that the manual operation of clicking on this tool for every new page being built takes a lot of manual interventions in getting the test done. Thus axe integrated automated accessibility audit becomes a one-point solution for any new web components to get built and tested for accessibility.

It includes cypress-axe within Devdependency of package. json as below:

```
"devDependencies": {
    "cypress": "^4.4.1",
    "cypress-axe": "^0.8.1",
},
```

Its installation can be done as follows:

```
npm i -D cypress-axe
```

Once cypress-axe is installed, it has to be imported in `index.js` file such as:

```
import 'cypress-axe'
```

Path: cypress\support

Once index has been updated, it is recommended to inject the browser when launching the uniform resource locator (URL) during the test execution. Since axe works inside the Document Object Model (DOM) properties of html website by scanning and auditing the complete page whenever instructed by automated tests, it is recommended to be called after `cy.visit` wherever it is written in the cypress framework:

```
export const loginOrangehrmPage = {
  launchPage(){
    cy.visit('/')
      .injectAxe();
  },
}
```

Path: cypress\pageobjects\LoginOrangehrm_PageObjects.js

Hence, this method has been called from page object javascript file; it is straight forward to be used in a step definition for accessibility testing:

```
Given('I open homepage', () => {
  loginOrangehrmPage.launchPage();
});
```

Path: cypress\support\step_definitions\login_steps_orangehrm.js

Remember that calling this launchPage will not perform the accessibility audit for the page; rather, it will just launch the website with `.visit` and inject the axe tool inside it. The remaining audit part has to be written in methods such as below:

```
allyAuditAxe(){
    cy.checkA11y(null, null, terminalLog);
}
```

Path: cypress\pageobjects\LoginOrangehrm_PageObjects.js

This method can be called in a step definition such as below:

```
Given('I perform accessibility audit using axe',
() => {
  loginOrangehrmPage.allyAuditAxe();
});
```

Now, we have got necessary step definitions to be used in a cucumber-based Behaviour Driven Development (BDD) file as below:

```
Feature: Login Page Accessibility Verification
on website

 Scenario: check login fields and perform
accessibility checks
   Given I open homepage
   And I perform accessibility audit using axe
```

Chapter 3

Running Cypress Tests in Docker

The container technology is getting matured with the latest docker versions along with the docker toolbox for Windows machines (except Mac OS, docker toolbox is easily installable for the majority of Windows versions).

Docker containers allow developers to create, deploy and run applications faster and quicker whenever they need them to be tested. With the traditional methods, application code is developed in the specific code environments such as Windows, Mac OS, linux operating systems, etc. When this code is transferred to different test environment for testing purpose or deployment needs, it results in defects or errors. For example, a developer transfers code from a desktop Mac computer to a Virtual Machine (VM) for deployment or from a Mac OS laptop to Windows machine for getting it tested. Containerisation eliminates this issue by bundling or grouping the application code along with Cypress test code and the related configuration files, libraries and dependencies required for the application to run. This container (single package of software) is abstracted away from the traditional host operating systems, no matter they are Windows, Mac or Linux or something else and then it becomes portable to run across any needed platform or cloud or free of environment-related errors or bugs.

Containers are often referred to as 'lightweight' since they get development and test code together along with configurations, share the machine's operating system kernel and do not require the overhead of sharing or associating a dedicated operating system within each application of code and test. So, Cypress tests just need two mandatory files for docker to run anywhere—dockerfile and. dockerignore (optionally docker-compose).

Docker file provides the options to add configuration; Details such as cypress.io browsers, node version (to be invoked) and the docker container instructions (to create working directory to copy the scripts) are required to be updated in container directory to run the tests.

dockerfile:

```
FROM cypress/browsers:node13.6.0-chrome80-ff72
# make directory inside container
RUN mkdir /cyTests
WORKDIR /cyTests
# copy cypress code from host to container
COPY. /cyTests
# perform installation
RUN npm install
RUN npm link
RUN npm link cypress-cucumber-preprocessor
RUN npm install through
# execute the tests
RUN npm run sanitytest:mochawesomereport
```

.dockerignore file (in. dockerignore file name) lists out any folder structure which is not required to get stored in a container. Specifically, folders such as videos and node_ modules can be mentioned in the. dockerignore file to avoid the huge file size.

.dockerignore file:

```
node_modules
```

If you are using test code without a development or application code to run automated tests, please make sure that dockerfile and. dockerignore file are added to the root of the project and once docker toolbox is opened, please build the code to run tests with the command below:

```
docker build -t cypress
```

Sample test results are given here in Figure 3.1:

Docker compose (in docker-compose.yml format) is a key file if you are deploying the development code to test. Build, environment and port details are required to invoke the services of the application to be tested.

```
# e2e/docker-compose.yml from repo
# https://github.com/bahmutov/
cypress-open-from-docker-compose
version: '3.2'
services:
```

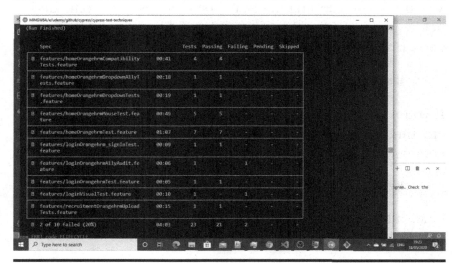

Figure 3.1   Docker View

```
# this is the web application we are going to
test
# sentimentalyzer:
#  build:. ./
#  environment:
#    - PORT=8123
# Cypress container
cypress:
  # the Docker image to use from https://github.
com/cypress-io/cypress-docker-images
    image: "cypress/included:4.0.2"
    #depends_on:
    #  - sentimentalyzer
    environment:
      # pass base url to test pointing at the web
application
      - CYPRESS_baseUrl=https://opensource-demo.
orangehrmlive.com
      # share the current folder as volume to avoid
copying
    working_dir: /e2e
    volumes:
      -. /:/e2e
```

When you are running the tests first time, use the command below in the right path of the project folder to build the image and bring the container up:

```
docker-compose up
```

If you want to run the application and test in docker at any time after the first run, you can invoke it by using the command below:

```
Docker start <container_id>
```

Once all the tests get completed in both the ways, please stop the docker container with the command below:

```
Docker stop <container_id>
```

Best Practices While Handling Cypress Tests in Docker

At any time during the docker-based test execution, if you want to check the complete container status of actively running containers and stopped containers, it can be checked by the command below:

```
docker ps -a
```

It is highly recommended to perform docker compose commands for the regular tests as follows:
Start all the services to run tests automatically.

```
docker-compose start
```

Stop all the services when tests are completed and not needed to keep them active.

```
docker-compose stop
```

If you want to delete all the test run history and records except the images, you can run the command below to bring the docker compose down:

```
docker-compose down
```

Since images are still not deleted, you can perform the command below to reuse the same scripts and images:

```
docker-compose up
```

But, these two commands such as up and down need to be used only when the test records need to be deleted in extraordinary circumstances. If they are performed regularly, there will not be any insights and statistics stored for the test reports.

Chapter 4

Test Reports

Mocha Awesome Reporter and Allure Reporter are useful reports, which can be integrated along with Cypress tests.

Mocha Awesome Reports

Installation: npm install -g mochawesome-report-generator
    Once the installation is completed, package.json gets the latest installed tool listed. This can be cross-checked. Otherwise, Mocha Awesome Report needs to get installed and updated in `package.json` file as below:

```
"devDependencies": {
  "mocha": "^5.2.0",
  "mocha-gherkin": "0.2.0",
  "mochawesome": "^3.1.2",
  "mochawesome-merge": "^2.1.0",
  "mocha-allure-reporter": "1.4.0",

},
"dependencies": {
  "mochawesome-report-generator": "4.1.0",
},
```

Note: Both mocha-allure-reporter and mochawesome-report-generator are primarily used for Allure Reporting (let us read it at the end of this chapter to compare and understand along with Mocha Awesome Reporting).

When the installation is completed, it is recommended to add a script to run tests with Mocha Report configuration within `package.json` file:

```
"scripts": {
  "test:mochawesomereport": "cypress run -r
mochawesome -s cypress/integration/features/*.
feature"
  }
```

As installation and script both steps have been completed, we have to get the configuration for the actual Mocha Report to the saved in a format such as this:

Reporter-options as stated in https://www.npmjs.com/package/mochawesome-report-generator

Use them in a `.mocharc.js` file:

```
module.exports = {
  reporter: 'node_modules/mochawesome',
  'reporter-option': [
      'overwrite=true',
      'reportTitle=My\ Custom\ Title',
      'showPassed=false'
  ],
};
```

So, I have got it configured under \cypress\config folder on two files:

`qa.json` file under \cypress\config states that I don't want to overwrite each Mocha Report when more than one tests run and more than one Mocha Reports are produced; hence, the results are produced in both json and html format. The qa file is configured to get the URL updated if I want to get it posted to any URL where developers and stakeholders are interested to have a look (through base URL).

```json
{
    "baseUrl": "https://qa.my",
    "reporter": "mochawesome",
    "reporterOptions": {
        "overwrite": false,
        "html": true,
        "json": true
    },
    "env": {
        "ENVIRONMENT": "qa",
        "CYPRESS_RETRIES": 2
    },
    "chromeWebSecurity": false,
    "requestTimeout": 30000,
    "defaultCommandTimeout": 60000,
    "numTestsKeptInMemory": 10,
    "pageLoadTimeout": 120000
}
```

Similarly, `staging.json` is updated with Mocha Report configurations at `\cypress\config`:

```json
{
    "baseUrl": "https://staging.com",
    "reporter": "mochawesome",
    "reporterOptions": {
        "overwrite": false,
        "html": true,
        "json": true
    },
    "env": {
        "ENVIRONMENT": "staging",
        "CYPRESS_RETRIES": 2
    },
    "chromeWebSecurity": false,
    "requestTimeout": 30000,
    "defaultCommandTimeout": 60000,
    "numTestsKeptInMemory": 10,
    "pageLoadTimeout": 120000
}
```

When scripts are configured in `package.json` file, it is easy to call the test from the terminal of Integrated Development Environment (IDE). If you are using visual studio code as an IDE to write scripts, it is easy to click on 'Terminal' to open new terminal and type the line of code to run the tests (headless in electron browser) using Mocha Report:

```
npm run test:mochawesomereport
```

During the test execution, terminal gives the complete test status live such as below:

```
PS E:\Udemy\github\cypress\cypress-test-
techniques> npm run sanitytest:mochawesomereport
> cypress-test-techniques-udemy@1.4.0
sanitytest:mochawesomereport E:\Udemy\github\
cypress\cypress-test-techniques
> cypress run -r mochawesome -s cypress/
integration/features/homeOrangehrmTest.feature
   (Run Starting)
   Cypress:     4.4.1
   Browser:     Electron 80 (headless)
   Specs:       1 found (features\
homeMainPageTest.feature)
   Searched:    cypress\integration\features\
homeMainPageTest.feature
   Running:   features\homeMainPageTest.feature
(1 of 1)
 Home Page Test on MainPage website
   √ Check valid home page tabs display
(7490ms)
       √ Click on Admin Tab of home page (5896ms)
       √ Double Click on Admin Tab of home page
(5705ms)
       √ Right Click on Admin Tab of home page
(4645ms)
       √ Check all employees on PIM Tab (5475ms)
       √ Uncheck all employees on PIM Tab (5696ms)
       √ Select Sales Manager in employees list on
PIM Tab (5420ms)
```

```
    7 passing (41s)

[mochawesome] Report JSON saved to E:\Udemy\
github\cypress\cypress-test-techniques\
mochawesome-report\mochawesome_017.json

[mochawesome] Report HTML saved to E:\Udemy\
github\cypress\cypress-test-techniques\
mochawesome-report\mochawesome_017.html

  (Results)
   Tests:          7
   Passing:         7
   Failing:        0
   Pending:         0
   Skipped:        0
   Screenshots:    0
   Video:       true
   Duration:    41 seconds
   Spec Ran:      features\homeMainPageTest.
feature
   Duration:    41 seconds
   Spec Ran:      features\homeMainPageTest.
feature
  (Video)
  -  Started processing:  Compressing to 32 CRF
    Compression progress:   47%
    Compression progress:   92%
  -  Finished processing: E:\Udemy\github\
cypress\cypress-test-techniques\cypress\vid
(22 seconds)
                  eos\features\homeMainPageTest.
feature.mp4
  (Run Finished)

    Spec                          Tests  Passing
Failing  Pending  Skipped
   √  features\homeMainPageTest.feature  00:41
7      7    -      -      -
   √  All specs passed!            00:41    7
7      -      -      -
```

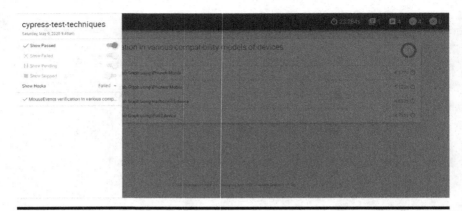

Figure 4.1   Test report using mocha

When the tests are completely executed, results of json file and html-based Mocha Reports are stored at \ `mochawesome-report`.

Mocha Awesome Reports come with the settings to enable or disable pass, fail, pending and skipped tests as shown in Figure 4.1.

Once the report is opened, it can be viewed along with the particular steps which are passed or failed such as below in Figure 4.2:

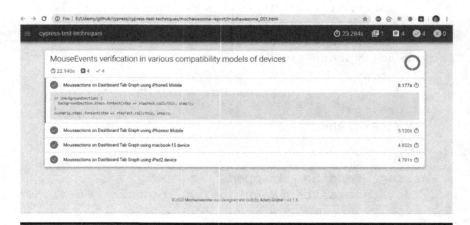

Figure 4.2   Test report expanded view

Mocha Allure Reports

If Mocha is already installed, please use:

```
npm install mocha-allure-reporter
```

If Mocha is not yet installed, try like a normal reporter installation model:

```
mocha --reporter mocha-allure-reporter
```

Once the installation is completed, `package.json` gets the latest installed tool listed. This can be cross-checked. Otherwise, Mocha Allure Report needs to be updated in `package.json` file as below:

```
   "devDependencies": {
   "mocha-allure-reporter": "1.4.0"

   },
   "dependencies": {
     "mochawesome-report-generator": "4.1.0"
   },
```

When the installation is completed, it is recommended to add a script to run tests with Mocha Report configuration within `package.json` file:

```
 "scripts": {
 "test:allurereport": "cypress run -b chrome -r
 mocha-allure-reporter -s cypress/integration/
 features/*.feature",
    "sanitytest:allurereport": "cypress run -b
 chrome -r mocha-allure-reporter -s cypress/
 integration/features/Test.feature",
    "generatereport": "allure generate allure-
 results --clean -o allure-report && allure open
 allure-report",
  }
```

Now, the test report generation of Allure Reports is two-step process:

If you want to run the entire test to get Allure Reports, perform these two commands:

```
npm run test:allurereport
```

Once this is completed, try this:

```
npm run generatereport
```

If you want to run any specific test to get Allure Reports, mention the test path in sanitytest:allurereport line within the script section of `package.json` and perform these two commands:

```
npm run sanitytest:allurereport
```

Once this is completed, try this:

```
npm run generatereport
```

test:allurereport and sanitytest:allurereport are the names I have provided to my tests. These can be amended to run more specific test scenarios or group of tests to produce results such as below:

```
npm run functionaltest:allurereport
npm run accessibilitytest:allurereport
npm run compatibilitytest:allurereport
```

Once the tests are executed using Allure Reporting, the reports can be generated using npm run generatereport. The test results are produced in a server with IP: Port to share the URL to launch the test results such as in Figure 4.3:

Figure 4.3   Allure report display view

Observation

Allure reports are lucrative and eye-catchy when it comes to fewer tests. In my experience, I have done tests for 300 to 500 features as a massive regression test pack and majority of the time, Allure Report took nearly three+ hours to generate a test report. Due to the nature of dense test results, it was not convenient for me to wait for additional hours to just generate one file of test report.

So, Mocha Reporting is thin and fast when multiple tests are used as a part of test execution and it has clear split between the test json files; hence, failed tests can be handpicked and selective json/html reports can be shared with the stakeholders to get the defect fixed in few minutes.

Chapter 5

Cypress Tests in Jenkins

Writing automation frameworks and configuring them to run in CI/CD model is the best practice in order to schedule tests and create dependency between development code and test code; hence, every change of development code can get the test code to run on top of it to find any failure. This is possible while creating test code-based pipeline; QA has to mention the pipeline name of the development code pipeline. Hence, any change or deployment to development code will kick start the test code. In our case, Cypress tests run in scheduled Jenkins pipeline to produce results, which are even sent as emails to the stakeholders.

Let us understand how to configure the Jenkins commands to run Cypress tests in Jenkins pipelines.

Step 1: Jenkins Installation

In organisations, Jenkins can be installed in virtual environments by DevOps Engineers and QAs can be provided with the URL to access Jenkins with valid user id and password. Whereas, if you are thinking to install and run Jenkins by youself, it can be installed in any laptop and the pipeline can be configured too, as shown in Figures 5.1, 5.2, 5.3 and Figure 5.4.

Figure 5.1 Jenkins installation step

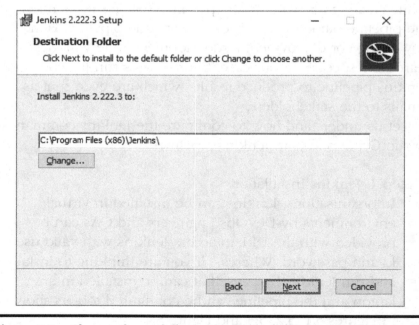

Figure 5.2 Choose the path for Jenkins installation in computer

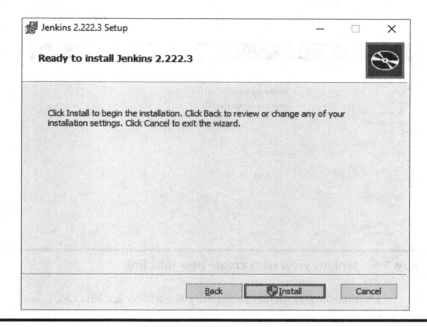

Figure 5.3   Install button on the setup process

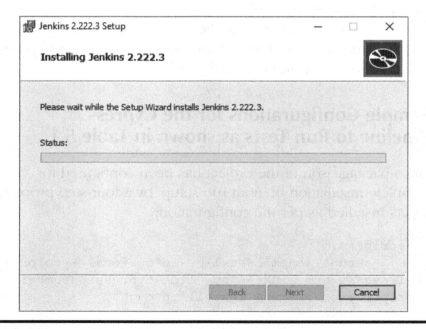

Figure 5.4   Jenkins installation status

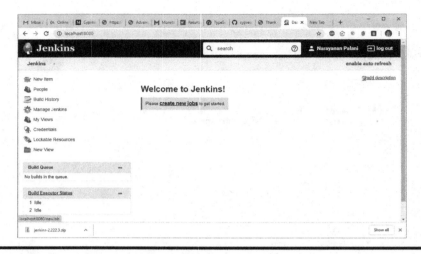

Figure 5.5   Jenkins view with create new jobs link

Download Jenkins from https://www.jenkins.io/
download/.

Once Jenkins is installed in a local machine, it can be
accessed through http://localhost:8080/.

Step 2: Creating New Jobs

Once Jenkins is installed, the simplest option is to click
'Create new jobs' to start creating a testing job for Cypress
tests as shown in Figure 5.5 and 5.6.

Sample Configurations for the Cypress Pipeline to Run Tests as shown in Table 5.1

Since package.json of the project has been configured for
complete installation of 'npm run setup' by a four-step process,
it gets installed as per the configuration:

```
"scripts": {
    "setup": "npm install --no-optional --color-
always && npm link && npm link cypress-cucumber-
preprocessor && npm install through",

}
```

Figure 5.6   New job details in jenkins

Table 5.1   Configurations sample for cypress test pipeline within jenkins

Description	Cypress Testing Framework
(Check) Github Project Project URL:	https://github.com/narayananpalani/cypress-test-techniques/
Source Code Management: Git Repositories	https://github.com/narayananpalani/cypress-test-techniques
Source Code Management: Git Credentials	None
Branches to build:	*/master
Build Triggers: (Check) GitHub hook trigger for GITScm polling	
Build Execute Windows Batch Command	npm run setup
Execute Windows Batch Command	npm run test:mochawesomereport

Click on 'Save' and 'Apply' buttons to save the changes to the pipeline configurations and get it ready; the next step is to click on 'Build Now' button to run the tests and see how the tests are getting executed remotely in Jenkins.

Chapter 6

Behaviour Driven Development (BDD)-based Feature File Writing Techniques using Cypress.io and Cucumber

Example:

```
Given, a user is provided with valid
authentication credentials of test website.
When user tries to login with valid credentials
on test website
Then the user should be displayed with home page
of test website successfully.
```

Now, let us understand the business scenario, which makes the projects to think that BDD is the right choice for their teams to write user stories.

When beginning with a new digital agile project, it is possible to take a decision on BDD when,

- The business can decide outcomes for features
- The developers know on types of components to build
- There is business understanding of technical issues and challenges to deal as technical spikes

During project initiation phase, epics are written for the features at high level and disaggregated further to several user stories preferably in Gherkin format.

Test automation architects can decide to reuse the same Gherkin lines of user stories into test repository or re-write further to make them more elaborate

In the example provided above, gherkin based cucumber tests can be re-used hence those steps will help in connecting to Cypress step definitions. So it can be re-used such as below:

```
Feature: Login Test on test website

 Scenario: Check valid signIn attempt with valid
user and password credentials
   Given I open Test website
   When I SignIn as valid user
   Then the user name should be displayed

 Scenario: Check invalid signIn attempt with
invalid user and valid password credentials
   Given I open Test website
   When I SignIn with incorrect user-name
   Then the error message should be displayed

 Scenario: Check invalid signIn attempt with
valid user and invalid password credentials
   Given I open Test website
   When I SignIn with incorrect password
   Then the error message should be displayed
```

```
Scenario:  Check invalid signIn attempt with
valid user and no password credentials
   Given I open Test website
   When I SignIn with username without password
   Then the error message should be displayed

Scenario: Check invalid signIn attempt with
valid password without username credentials
   Given I open Test website
   When I SignIn with password without username
   Then the error message should be displayed
```

Even though the objective of the tests is to match the requirements provided in three lines in Gherkin format, it needs more negative tests to support the functionality being developed.

As a next step, 'Given I open Test website' can be converted to a valid Cypress code by adding a step definition to it.

Under support/step_definitions folder, tester can create a new .js file to write this step definition as follows:

```
Given( 'I open Test website', () => {
   loginPage.launchPage();
});
```

LaunchPage is nothing but a function inside page object pattern of loginPage. Hence, it can be written within '.pageobjects/' folder as `loginPage.js` file:

```
launchPage(){
   cy.visit('/');
},
```

Alternative:

If you are thinking to perform accessibility code audit later in the stages of testing, it is recommended to inject axe plugin as a code while launching the web page by

```
launchPage(){
   cy.visit('/')
```

```
      .injectAxe();
    },
```

As a best practice to Cypress test repositories, the primary URLs of the application are to be managed centrally from `cypress.json`. Thus, the `cy.visit` (in the code above) has been provided with the suffix of the URL, which we need to perform tests.

So, the `cypress.json` needs the primary URL path to be mentioned in the route within the `cypress.json` file:

```
"baseUrl": "<provide base url here>",
```

In this way, `cypress.json` sends the URL prefix to launchPage function within the page objects and the launchPage function adds the suffix as '/' and gives it to `cy.visit` to launch the page. Eventually, this launchPage is called within the step definition, which is linked to Cucumber Gherkin tests with the 'Given' format of code under support/ step_definition; So page launching javascript code has been triggered to Cypress server through simple Cucumber Gherkin lines. Finally, all these are managed to launch the web page within the Cypress running interface within a few milliseconds!

How is Cypress Different from Selenium while Launching the Websites?

Selenium can be scripted by calling the URLs centrally in separate js files when using `world.js` and `cuke.js` in WebdriverIO-based selenium JavaScript projects. But, the page can be launched only through browser drivers, which receive the selenium comments and talk to browsers through a series of HTTP requests. Hence, there is a time delay involved by the nature of selenium architecture. If the browser is stale or not responsive due to the page load time, QA will not know the test failure until the tests get completed. So, the wait mechanism needs to be adjusted by calling explicit wait instead of implicit waits in selenium commands to deal with this complexity.

Cypress has been developed by considering these complexities hence Cypress commands do not need mentioning of any wait commands. Yes, that's right! By default, Cypress performs a retry function to redo the action or event on the web page, if there is a time delay in loading the web page. It fails only after retry and there is a four-second default timeout when there is a delay or timeout occurs, which can be altered by code, if required.

So, Cypress tests provide consistent results and avoid flaky tests, which are common in Selenium test frameworks.

WebdriverIO launches the website through `browser.url` (URL) and this can be done through Cypress as `cy.visit` (URL); WebdriverIO (Selenium's JavaScript version) can be scripted in asynchronous mode or synchronous mode by configuring sync=true or false at `cuke.conf` level in configurations, but it is not possible in Cypress for a valid reason: Cypress tests run swiftly and provide results in no time; hence, asynchronous is by default expected in Cypress tests. So, there is no need for Cypress to support synchronous way of writing scripts in the recent years.

Chapter 7

Differences Between Selenium and Cypress.io

Since 2007, Selenium has been transformed from Integrated Development Environment (IDE) and Remote Control (RC) versions to stable Webdriver to facilitate programming language support across Java, JavaScript (through wdio), C#, Python, Ruby and few other languages. Thus, the development teams are finding it suitable to build their source code and test code parallelly in the same programming language. But, there are underlying challenges to the architecture due to *flaky tests* (not providing consistent results every time for the source code which has no changes), *time-consuming browser drivers* (taking ages to return the results back to Selenium to process the reports) and *complex maintenance of Selenium code when API testing is involved* (since Selenium doesn't provide support to application interfaces, but there are various tools such as apickli to enhance API scripts to run along with Selenium).

All these problems have been addressed by Cypress.io. It provides super-fast tests by avoiding browser drivers in the framework; it facilitates consistent test results since the tests run inside the browser rather than interacting with the browsers through drivers and spending extra time (tools such as Selenium, Unified Functional Testing or UFT) and finally, it provides in-built support for application programming interface through XMLHttpRequest (XHR) libraries; hence, there is no need to be dependant on different tools to write mocks for outgoing dependencies and stubs for incoming dependencies. So, Cypress.io has become a favourite of developers with limited browser support until 2019 by running tests in Google Chrome and Electron. During 2020, it has released version 4.0.0 that supports Mozilla Firefox, Microsoft Edge, Google Chrome and Canary (latest features of Chrome released in Canary as Beta to try the user experience). Hence, Cypress.io allows the QAs to perform next generation tests (by testing along with Canary) to be prepared for future versions of browser to test against application source code.

In my industry experience, I was looking for a stable end-to-end regression test engine for regression tests to run across various browsers and just test the user journeys, which was fulfilled by Selenium through WebdriverIO. But, I had no tool to test unit integration tests since many application issues are to be identified only at later stages such as system integration testing and user acceptance testing rather than finding them all during unit integration testing and system testing stages.

When I started using Cypress during 2018, it was easy to spot the application issues during unit integration testing itself; hence, the defects were prevented rather than spotted during system testing and system integration testing stages. As a step forward, Cypress versions 4.x and above are helping to test the applications through accessibility (using cypress-axe plugin), cross browser testing (using four different browser types at least) and visual regression; hence, defect prevention is brought early in the test life cycle as a best *shift left test approach*!

It is highly recommended to bring Cypress tests early in the life cycle and keep Selenium for integration testing (to address regression tests); hence, both tools can fit into test cycles to avoid duplication of tests and provide better defect prevention mechanism to application development!

Cypress is expected to stay as No.2 after Selenium tool users in the market according to the latest social media polls. But, it is a No.1 choice for projects with ReactJS-based or NodeJS front-end applications. On another note, the majority of the front-end applications are moving away from Java to JavaScript since 2016. So, it is evident that Cypress will grow to reach Selenium's No.1 rank and both tools will share the QA space equally to serve the testing projects based on the front-end application choices.

When the front-end application is written in JavaScript, developers need or recommend test code in JavaScript since the application code needs to be built as .js files and managed through npm packages (in node.js applications); hence, Cypress.io is an absolute JavaScript end-to-end scripting tool to fit this need. Additionally, developer's needs of mocks and stubs were addressed by various toolsets in the past and sometimes, it is hard to even script those mechanism to facilitate API testing, but all of these are supported through Cypress XHR by intercepting XMLHttpRequests. So, developers and testers prefer Cypress to Selenium since no other tool does this extended support of API testing along with functional testing in the current available open source toolsets.

Chapter 8

Cypress Cucumber Preprocessor Errors

Some Best Practices

Avoid using caret symbol ^ or tilde symbol ˜ in `package.json` file for toolsets.

- Note that ˜ version **"Approximately equivalent to version"** will update the tool to all future patch versions, without incrementing the minor version. ˜1.3.4 will use releases from 1.3.4 to <1.4.0.
- ^ version **"Compatible with version"** will update the tool to all future minor/patch versions, without incrementing the major version. ^2.4.4 will use releases from 2.4.4 to <3.0.0.

If you are seeing errors such as *Error: Cannot find module 'test/cypress/support/step_definitions/shared.js'*, it is due to incompatible version of Cucumber preprocessor giving error while referring to step definitions within the framework, as shown in Figure 8.1.

Figure 8.1   cypress cucumber preprocessor error during the test execution

In order to fix the conflicts, please reverse the tool version of Cypress Cucumber preprocessor to one of the stable version (earlier version) to run `npm install` and the tests once again to recover from the error.

This is one of the known path-breaking changes introduced from the code version 1.2.0 of Cypress Cucumber preprocessor as per the instructions in Github:

https://github.com/TheBrainFamily/cypress-cucumber-preprocessor/issues/78

Chapter 9

Device Compatibility Testing Using Cypress.io

In my experience, I had a situation to order essential items from an online grocery store during the peak of pandemic in 2020. It was 1.20 AM and that is the first time I managed to get a delivery slot available to attach to my shopping cart to order the items to get delivered in a near possible date. Unfortunately, I used Google Pixel2 XL to click on shopping cart to make a payment and the payment failed almost all the time when I tried. After four times of retry which were failed, I had to call the bank to figure out that the payment was not yet made through any of the attempts. I realised that the QA has missed the testing of payment integration to the shopping cart using mobile devices. So, I used a laptop with Google Chrome immediately to make the payment and it went through seamlessly and I got the order delivered on time. Hence, the lesson is 'device compatibility testing' using view ports such as Google Pixel2 XL. Do you think I have left it there? No.

I wrote to the grocery shop when the sellers requested for a feedback through automatic review emailer with clear example stating the QA's miss of performing device compatibility tests along with payment interfaces during SIT phase of their shopping web page. Thus, they have taken it seriously (looks like) and fixed it which I figured out when I made a payment through Google Pixel 2 XL after two months of the incident.

Test Strategy of Device Compatibility Tests

It is not a good solution to wait until SIT phase to test device compatibility in order to find defects. The reason is QAs wait until API microservices are getting built in order to test those compatibilities with the back-end system connectivity since no enough stubbing options are available beforehand. This situation no more exists when Cypress.io has arrived with XHR microservices testing along with the various viewport support for mobile and tablet compatibility testing right from the same app of Cypress, which is used for functional testing on web browsers!

Cypress.io supports a wide variety of viewports, which can be referred from the documentation at:

https://docs.cypress.io/api/commands/viewport. html#Arguments

Even when there is a new release of a mobile device out and QA needs to get it tested, it is possible with Cypress as long as the height and width are known to enter in the configuration here:

```
cy.viewport(width,height)
```

Implementation

BDD feature file at `cypress\integration\features\*. feature`:

```
Scenario: Verify Dashboard Tab Graph using iPad2
device
        Given I open homepage
        When I SignIn as user
```

```
        When I see the page in iPad2 version
        When I perform move actions on dashboard
graph
        Then text insights displayed below
dashboard successfully
```

Step definition at `cypress\support\step _ definitions\*.js`:

```
When('I see the page in iPad2 version', () => {
   homeOrangehrmPage.viewPortipad2()
})
```

Page object at `cypress\pageobjects\*PageObjects.js`:

```
   viewPortipad2 () {
      cy.viewport('ipad-2')
   },
```

In this way, viewports can be handled in a Page Object Pattern as well as reused across the framework to test the needed pages in a particular compatibility mode.

Cypress.io Test Strategy

Testing device compatibility is possible with Cypress.io in early phases of the life cycle and it is as simple as developing the page locally and run in various device viewports to see the behaviour of UI components in no time! Also, the same tests can be rerun when microservices are integrated to those web pages.

Hence, fixing a compatibility defect is cheap and easy while developing the pages with the help of Cypress.io. Also, rerunning those scripts with microservices (by removing stubs and adding actual API calls) helps in finding failures in API requests/responses at an earlier stage.

Some Myths

Generally, there are assumptions about compatibility and accessibility tests that they are one and the same. It is completely wrong. Compatibility tests help in finding issues when the page is loaded in mobile view or tablet view, whereas accessibility tests help in finding issues when users with disabilities access these pages using screen readers or assistive technologies such as ZoomText. Since both are different in nature, both compatibility and accessibility testing are 'must' for any customer using web applications.

Chapter 10

Disabled Object Verification Through Force: True

Example code:

```
uploadResumeForce () {
  const fileName = 'ResumeIncorrectExt.png'

  cy.readFile('.//cypress//fixtures//Resume.
txt').then(function (fileContent) {
    cy.xpath(uploadBtn_RecrTab).attachFile({
fileContent, fileName, mimeType: 'application/
txt' })
    cy.xpath(uploadBtn_RecrTab).dblclick({
force: true })
  })
},
```

In the example code above, upload button is used to upload resume of the candidates to add them to the HR Recruitment portal. There are selected file types acceptable in this application such as .docx, .doc, .odt, .pdf, .rtf, .txt, but I want to try forcing by adding a .png file. It is a negative test to make sure that no exceptions or errors are thrown in the back-end and at the same time, it is appropriate while handling an incorrect file. So, I can force the upload button to click by click({force: true}) or I can use dblclick({force: true}) to double click on the upload button. Even when the button is disabled, it will force the object to get it clicked to check the behaviour.

Chapter 11

Upload File Using Cypress.io

The primary challenge in this mechanism is that direct support is not provided by open source test engines. Hence, any error or exceptions occurred during this integration of toolsets to verify upload mechanism (as an example) may be limited to a few possible combinations instead of trying various negative test scenarios.

Also, it is extremely limited to run regression tests when message validations are involved and those messages are sourced from back-end systems. Hence, placing these tests is limited to system integration tests or regression tests. Since these tests are automated at the right edge of the project life cycle, finding any defects at this stage is expensive to get fixed (since there will be a need to run regression tests after the fixes brought into the latest code base).

Following is the sample line of code using Selenium and Sikuli[2] in Java Programming:

```
package com.sikuli.Sample;
import org.sikuli.script.Pattern;
import org.sikuli.script.Screen;
import org.openqa.selenium.chrome.ChromeDriver;
```

```
import org.openqa.selenium.By;
import org.openqa.selenium.WebDriver;
import org.sikuli.script.FindFailed;

public class SikuliSampleScripts {
  public static void main(String[] args) throws
FindFailed {
    System.setProperty("webdriver.chrome.
driver", "D:\\chromedriver.exe");
    String filepath = "Path\\Files\\";
    String inputFilePath = "Path\\Files\\";
    Screen s = new Screen();
    Pattern fileInputTextBox = new
Pattern(filepath + "Resume.txt");
    Pattern openButton = new Pattern(filepath +
"Resume.txt");
    WebDriver driver;
    driver = new ChromeDriver();
    driver.get("Web URL");
    //Automation tool perform click action on
Browse button to handle windows pop up by Sikuli
    driver.findElement(By.xpath(".//*
[@id='addCandidate_resume']")).click();
    s.wait(fileInputTextBox, 20);
    s.type(fileInputTextBox, inputFilePath +
"Resume.txt");
    s.click(openButton);
    driver.close();
```

This function looks straightforward to perform user click on the upload button to upload the text file. But, there are some negative experiences in the past such as:

```
screen src = new Screen();
Match addFile= src.find("Path\\Capture.PNG");


FindFailed: can not find Path\Capture.PNG on the
screen.
Line? , in File?
```

```
at org.sikuli.script.Region.
handleFindFailed(Region.java:420)
    at org.sikuli.script.Region.wait(Region.
java:511)
    at org.sikuli.script.Region.find(Region.
java:381)
    at pagefactory.profile_section.
ResearchandExp_pageFact.click_Attach_
Documents(ResearchandExp_pageFact.java:195)
    at TestCase.
ResearchandExpertise_TC.attach_Document_to_
Research(ResearchandExpertise_TC.java:311)
    at sun.reflect.NativeMethodAccessorImpl.
invoke0(Native Method)
```

This issue occurred whenever the image file is not loaded to the source location within three seconds and Sikuli fails to find such file in limited time due to default timeout.

Let us understand the same file upload mechanism in Cypress in the most simplest way.

Pre-requisites:

Install cypress-file-upload by

```
npm install –save-dev cypress-file-upload
```

Once installed, update the package.json with the line on this tool with a latest version like the below:

```
"cypress-file-upload": "4.0.6",
```

Update commands.js at the file path .\cypress\ support\commands.js with an import command[1] such as:

```
import 'cypress-file-upload'
```

Step 1:

Place the text file in fixtures folder: .\cypress\fixtures

Step 2:

Write a small function on the upload mechanism by defining the object, read the file through Cypress and then use a function to attach file and upload using mimetype on the path: .\cypress\pageobjects.

This file upload can be performed in Cypress using the following sample script:

```
const uploadBtn_RecrTab = '//*
[@id=\'addCandidate_resume\']'
uploadResume () {
    const fileName = 'Resume.txt'

    cy.readFile('.//cypress//fixtures//Resume.
txt').then(function (fileContent) {
        cy.xpath(uploadBtn_RecrTab).attachFile({
fileContent, fileName, mimeType: 'application/
txt' })
        cy.xpath(uploadBtn_RecrTab).click()
    })
},
```

Step 3:

This function (uploadResume) can be called to a step definition at path: .\cypress\support\ step _ definitions

```
Then('I uploaded the resume forcefully', () => {
  recOrangehrmPage.uploadResumeForce()
})
```

Step 4:

It can then be used in a feature file such as the below: Path: .\cypress\integration\features

```
    Feature: Upload functionality tests of home
page
```

```
        Scenario: Upload resume in recruitment tab
of the Orangehrm* website
        Given I open homepage
        When I SignIn as user
        And I click on Recruitment tab of home page
        And I click on Add button to add resume
        And I uploaded the resume successfully
```

The primary benefit of Cypress.io is the inbuilt feature to help uploading files using functions; hence, no new tools or packages are required to get this upload mechanism tested. One of the major advantage of this approach is to enable developers to test this feature even when the back-end systems and microservices are not fully ready!

Cypress XHR supports the stubbing options to tweak the responses with the right error messages to verify the behaviour of the upload button while developing the page.

References

[1] https://www.guru99.com/sikuli-tutorial.html.
[2] https://stackoverflow.com/questions/31267391/can-not-find-image-path-in-upload-document-script-using-sikuli-with-webdriver.

---

* **Note**
OrangeHRM Open Source is a free and open source HR software and it has been given as an application example for constructing the automation tests in this book (Reference: https://www.orangehrm.com/services/)

Chapter 12

Conditional Tests: A Comparison Between Selenium and Cypress.io

During the Selenium tests, after a certain period of test execution cycle, test results go flaky with large failure rate due to the inconsistency between the page load times and they are not going to be the same when the tests are rerun. Here comes the need for conditions[1] such as isClickable, isDisplayed and isHidden.

Let us take an example of isClickable in Selenium:

```
WebDriverWait wait = new
WebDriverWait(Scenario1Test.driver, 10);
WebElement element =
wait.until(ExpectedConditions.
elementToBeClickable(By.xpath("(//div
[@id='home'])")));
element.click();
```

These kinds of conditions help Selenium to wait for the buttons to be clickable and available to perform actions before actually clicking on the buttons. Similar approaches are followed on other user interactions such as text box inputs, select checkboxes, select dropdowns, etc.

These conditions such as isClickable are helpful to script along with explicit wait (better than implicit wait) in order to wait and run the tests; hence, the tests run for longer time than expected.

How do we find an element is - isClickable - isDisplayed -isHidden in Cypress?

'isClickable' kind of conditions are useful to go along with wait conditions in automation engines such as Selenium, whereas Cypress.io is a modern end-to-end automation tool to deal with the wait as inbuilt functionality. By default, Cypress.io waits for four seconds and it can be amended through configurations, but engineers do not require any other additional line of code to be written for the wait conditions when writing the framework using Cypress.io tests!

Since there is no necessity for a wait-related line of code in Cypress, there is no necessity to write conditions such as isClickable in Cypress. But, how do automated tests know whether the button or any object is clickable (when page load with delays) and how can the tests be performed on the exact time when the button gets loaded?

Let us take a step back and understand how Cypress performs retries[3] and waits for the commands.

Cypress.io retries[2] by default for commands such as get(), contains() and find(), but it does not perform retry for commands such as click(), which is the topic of discussion to compare with isClickable() of Selenium.

But, Cypress.io is smart enough to wait by default until the button is actionable. In another words, Cypress.io has inbuilt algorithm to deal with isClickable() within automation test engine. That's why we don't have any option to perform conditions such as isClickable() in Cyperssio. Thus, Cypress.io just simplifies the work for automation engineers and developers!

References

[1] https://stackoverflow.com/questions/38327049/
check-if-element-is-clickable-in-selenium-java.

[2] https://www.npmjs.com/package/cypress-plugin-retries.

[3] https://docs.cypress.io/guides/core-concepts/retry-ability.
html#Not-every-command-is-retried.

## Chapter 13

Testing Dropdowns Using Cypress.io

Selenium Usage (Java Programming)

```
String salesMgr="Sales Manager";
    if(driver.findElements(By.xpath("//*[@
id='empsearch_job_title']")).size() > 0){
    Select titleDropdown = new Select (driver.
findElement(By.id("jobTitle")));
    titleDropdown.selectByVisibleText(salesMgr);
}
```

If the dropdown is provided with a large list of items such as country code or in case of selecting a country from dropdown, choosing an item from the bottom of the list needs a lot of scroll down to the bottom.

Implementation

BDD Feature File

```
Feature: Dropdown functionality tests of home
page
```

```
Scenario: Select sales manager job title in
employees search list on PIM Tab
    Given I open homepage
    When I SignIn as user
    And I click on PIM tab of home page
    And I click on dropdown of jobtitle
    And I click on search button of pim tab
    Then search results should be displayed
successfully
```

Step Definition

```
When('I click on dropdown of jobtitle', () => {
    homeOrangehrmPage.jobTitleDropdown()
})
```

Page Objects and Functions

```
const jobTitleDropdown_pim = '//*[@
id=\'empsearch_job_title\']'
    jobTitleDropdown () {
        cy.get('select').xpath(jobTitleDropdown_pim)
            .select('Sales Manager').should('have.
value', '1')
    },
```

Alternatively, engineers can get the selection forced by the code below:

```
const jobTitleDropdown_pim = '//*[@
id=\'empsearch_job_title\']'
    jobTitleDropdown () {
        cy.get('select').xpath(jobTitleDropdown_pim)
            .select('Sales Manager', {force: true}).
should('have.value', '1')
    },
```

Benefits of Cypress.io in Dropdown Selection

Cypress.io runs the tests in a controlled browser setup and the tests run inside the browser with the help of Cypress, which also controls the DOM of the page display. Hence, there is less possibility for the dropdown selections to go wrong. Cypress has by default wait feature if there is a delay in loading the list inside dropdown while expanding the list by dropdown selection.

Chapter 14

BeforeEach and AfterEach Hooks

BeforeEach Hook

It is a root level hook to get the commands called before starting all the tests. Hence, it is recommended to use visit commands to launch a specific page before performing test validations.

It can be added to cypress\support\commands.js:

```
beforeEach(() => {
    // root-level hook
    // runs before every test
    cy.log('Tests Started');
    cy.visit("/");
})
```

cypress\integration\form.spec.js:

```
describe("Form test", () => {
    it("Can fill the form", () => {

        cy.get("form");
        cy.get('input[name="name"]')
        .type("Narayanan Palani")
```

```
            .should("have.value", "Narayanan Palani");

        cy.get('input[name="email"]')
        .type("np@dev.dev")
        .should("have.value", "np@dev.dev");

        cy.get("textarea")
        .type("Mind you if I ask some silly
question?")
        .should("have.value", "Mind you if I ask
some silly question?");

        cy.server();
        cy.route({
            url: "/users/**",
            method: "POST",
            response: { status: "Form saved!",
code: 201 }
        });

        cy.get("form").submit();

        cy.contains("Form saved!");
    });
});
```

AfterEach Hook

Instead of verifying individually, the codecan be grouped at last to get it executed at the end of every test.

Scenario 1: Running a tests with hooks
cypress\integration\form.spec.js:

```
describe("Form test", () => {

    it("Can fill the form", () => {

        cy.get("form");
        cy.get('input[name="name"]')
```

```
        .type("Narayanan Palani")
        .should("have.value", "Narayanan Palani");

        cy.get('input[name="email"]')
        .type("np@dev.dev")
        .should("have.value", "np@dev.dev");

        cy.get("textarea")
        .type("Mind you if I ask some silly
question?")
        .should("have.value", "Mind you if I ask
some silly question?");

        cy.server();
        cy.route({
          url: "/users/**",
          method: "POST",
          response: { status: "Form saved!", code:
201 }
        });

        cy.get("form").submit();


    });

    afterEach(() => {
      // runs after each test in the block
      cy.contains("Form saved!");
    })
});
```

Scenario 2

Running two tests with the same URL and the same
verification at the end can be done by updating the
beforeEach and afterEach hooks at the root level, i.e., at
commands.js file.

AfterEach can be controlled by adding it to `cypress\support\commands.js`:

```
beforeEach(() => {
    // root-level hook
    // runs before every test
    cy.log('Tests Started');
    cy.visit("/");
  });


 afterEach(() => {
    // runs after each test in the block
    cy.contains("Form saved!");
  })
```

Let us look at the two form filling tests.
`cypress\integration\form.spec.js`

```
describe("Form test", () => {

    it("Can fill the form", () => {

        cy.get("form");
        cy.get('input[name="name"]')
        .type("Narayanan Palani")
        .should("have.value", "Narayanan
Palani");

        cy.get('input[name="email"]')
        .type("np@dev.dev")
        .should("have.value", "np@dev.dev");

        cy.get("textarea")
        .type("Mind you if I ask some silly
question?")
        .should("have.value", "Mind you if I ask
some silly question?");

        cy.server();
```

```
        cy.route({
          url: "/users/**",
          method: "POST",
          response: { status: "Form saved!",
code: 201 }
        });

        cy.get("form").submit();


      });

});
```

cypress\integration\form.spec.negative.js:

```
describe("Form negative test", () => {

    it("Can fill the form", () => {

        cy.get("form");
        cy.get('input[name="name"]')
        .type("Mac O' Donald")
        .should("have.value", "Mac O' Donald");

        cy.get('input[name="email"]')
        .type("n*p@dev.dev")
        .should("have.value", "n*p@dev.dev");

        cy.get("textarea")
        .type("Mind you if I ask some silly
question on !£$%^?)(*")
        .should("have.value", "Mind you if I ask
some silly question on !£$%^?)(*");

        cy.server();
        cy.route({
          url: "/users/**",
          method: "POST",
```

```
            response: { status: "Form saved!",
code: 201 }
        });

        cy.get("form").submit();


    });

});
```

But, in these examples, both 'get form' and 'form submission' are written twice since there are two tests. It can be avoided by writing before and after for these tests to avoid duplication:

cypress\support\commands.js:

```
beforeEach(() => {
    // root-level hook
    // runs before every test
    cy.log('Tests Started');
    cy.visit("/");
    cy.get("form");
});

afterEach(() => {
    // runs after each test in the block
    cy.get("form").submit();
    cy.contains("Form saved!");
});
```

Let us look at the two form filling tests.
cypress\integration\form.spec.js:

```
describe("Form test", () => {

    it("Can fill the form", () => {
        cy.get('input[name="name"]')
        .type("Narayanan Palani")
        .should("have.value", "Narayanan Palani");
```

```
        cy.get('input[name="email"]')
        .type("np@dev.dev")
        .should("have.value", "np@dev.dev");

        cy.get("textarea")
        .type("Mind you if I ask some silly
question?")
        .should("have.value", "Mind you if I ask
some silly question?");

        cy.server();
        cy.route({
          url: "/users/**",
          method: "POST",
          response: { status: "Form saved!",
code: 201 }
        });

        });

});
```

cypress\integration\form.spec.negative.js:

```
describe("Form negative test", () => {

    it("Can fill the form", () => {
        cy.get('input[name="name"]')
        .type("Mac O' Donald")
        .should("have.value", "Mac O' Donald");

        cy.get('input[name="email"]')
        .type("n*p@dev.dev")
        .should("have.value", "n*p@dev.dev");

        cy.get("textarea")
        .type("Mind you if I ask some silly
question on !£$%^?)(*")
        .should("have.value", "Mind you if I ask
some silly question on !£$%^?)(*");
```

```
        cy.server();
        cy.route({
          url: "/users/**",
          method: "POST",
          response: { status: "Form saved!",
code: 201 }
        });
      });

});
```

What If We Want to Use Before() and After() Instead of BeforeEach() and AfterEach()?

If we run each test individually through npx Cypress open command, then each one gets executed as expected, whereas running all specs will fail after the first test because 'before' and 'after' are run only once. So, running the second test without performing form save results in appending the inputs written by the first test to the inputs of the second test; hence, assertions of the second test fail immediately.

Chapter 15

Generic Test Automation Architecture of Cypress.io

According to the generic Test Automation Architecture (gTAA) of ISTQB Advanced Test Automation Engineering syllabus, it is really useful to understand a test framework when constructing the advantages using gTAA view as shown in **Figure 15.1: General Test Automation Architecture (gTAA) according to the ISTQB®**.

The gTAA is structured into horizontal layers for the following:

■ Test generation
■ Test definition
■ Test execution
■ Test adaptation

The gTAA (Cypress.io) encompasses the following:

■ The test generation layer supports the manual or automated design of test cases for Cypress.io JavaScript tests. It provides the means for designing test cases; hence, an engineer can write BDD-based feature files to arrive at the manual design of the tests. Advanced

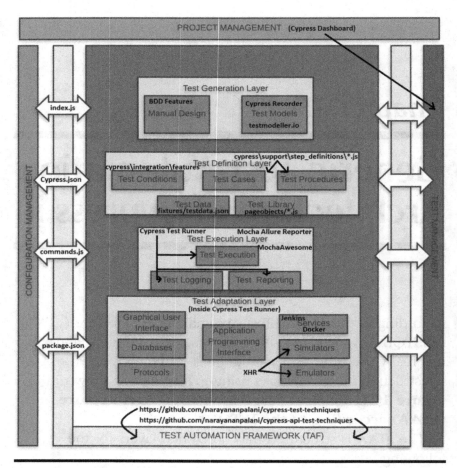

Figure 15.1 **General Test Automation Architecture (gTAA)**

tools such as **testmodeller.io** (*model based testing tool*) help in defining the model of Cypress tests that can be converted to Cypress test scripts direct from the high-level model. Similarly, **Cypress Recorder** is a kind of Google Chrome extension that makes the life easy by recording the automated test scripts for Cypress tests as automated design.

■ The test definition layer supports the definition and implementation of test suites and/or test cases in which **Cucumber** *features* (BDD feature files) provide the test conditions. It separates the test definition from the System Under Test (SUT) and/or test system technologies and tools. It contains means to define high-level and low-level tests, which are handled in the test data (using fixtures), test cases (`spec.js` along with step definitions), test procedures (`spec.js` along with step definitions) and test library components (using pageobjects)s or combinations thereof.

■ The test execution layer supports the execution of test cases through **Cypress Test Runner, Mocha Awesome** or through **Mocha Allure Reporting** and also supports test logging of the respective tools. It provides a test execution tool to execute the selected tests automatically and a logging and reporting component.

■ The test adaptation layer provides the necessary code to adapt the automated tests for the various components or interfaces of the SUT. It provides different adaptors for connecting to the SUT via APIs (through XHR of Cypress.io), protocols, services (such as docker, Jenkins) and others.

■ It also has interfaces for project management, test management through Cypress Dashboard (Licensed) and configuration management through `cypress.json`, `index.js` and `commands.js` in relation to test automation.

Setting Up A gTAA Along with SUT Using Cypress.io

Most often, engineers would start with the implementation of a Test Automation Solution (TAS) from bottom to top (GUI to feature files), but other approaches such as the automated test generation for manual tests can be useful as well (test-first approach of writing feature files, preparing Cypress tests and then designing GUI of the application). In general, it is advised to implement the TAS in incremental steps (e.g., in sprints) in order to use the TAS as soon as possible and to prove the added value of the TAS. Also, the proofs of concept are recommended as a part of test automation project.

Early implementation of Cypress.io test-first approach is advanced and brings the project towards defect prevention rather than defect identification through costly test cycles.

In my experience, writing BDD-based Cucumber Gherkin files helps in writing product features and test features simultaneously with detailed combinations. Hence, it gives the opportunity to write tests before starting the application development. Thus, writing those feature files into Cypress tests is straightforward to get constructed along with custom qa-selectors (object repository) to further enhance developing Graphical User Interface (GUI). So, UI and web component behaviour can be tested with the help of Cypress as both Unit Integration as well as System Integration Tests (if back-end microservices are available).

When back-end systems are not ready, Cypress helps in XHR API stubbing; hence, it facilitates testing of the user interactions with positive as well as negative tests such as error message verifications.

Test Generation Layer of Cypress.io

The test generation layer consists of tool support for the following:

- Manually designing feature file-based test cases in BDD mode or writing specification js files in Test Driven Development (TDD) mode
- Developing, capturing, or deriving test data within fixtures folder of Cypress test framework
- Automatically generating test cases (js step definitions) from models using Cypress recorder Google Chrome extensions that define the basic user interactions recorded

The components of this layer are used to:

- Edit and navigate test suite structures
- Relate test cases to test objectives or SUT requirements since most of the feature files written for product features in BDD format are generally reused
- Document the test design through ReadMe

For automated test generation, the following capabilities are possible through testmodeller.io:

- Ability to model the SUT tests using models in testmodeller.io
- Ability to define test directives and to configure/ parameterise test generation algorithms after capturing through testmodeller automation and generation through paths
- Ability to trace the generated tests back to the model (elements) to perform root cause analysis
- Updating test framework's need to resynchronise those updated objects back in the testmodeller

Refer and use the testmodeller.io generated Cypress tests at: https://github.com/CuriositySoftwareIreland/ TestModeller-CypressFramework

Try the online YouTube tutorial at: https://www.youtube. com/watch?v=8G-xhdnlxsI&feature=youtu.be

What is Not Possible Using Test Generation Layer of Cypress Tests?

Mock data: Any outgoing dependencies are known as mocks for the API services and as of July 2020, there is no possibility to mix the mocked data along with real API data to send through Cypress with the help of any model-based testing tools and it is something expected in the upcoming releases. So, tweaking headers, contract body may not be straightforward when models are used.

Autogenerate the framework: The entire Cypress framework can't be autogenerated with few clicks in any model-based testing tools and this has to be configured at code level for a better maintenance of the framework.

Parallel or grid tests: In the open source version of Cypress, parallel test execution is not possible if it gets executed locally. But, it is possible to run those parallel tests if configuring with cloud solutions such as BrowserStack.

Test Definition Layer of Cypress.io

Cypress provides tool support for the following:

- Specifying test cases (at a high and/or low level) (scripts can be referred at `integration\features folder`)
- Defining test data for low-level test cases through step definitions at `cypress\support\step _ definitions\*.js`
- Specifying test procedures for a test case or a set of test cases through `cypress.json`
- Defining test scripts for the execution of the test cases through `package.json`
- Providing access to test libraries as needed (for example in keyword-driven approaches) such as page object pattern through `cypress\pageobjects\*.js`

The components of this layer are used to:

- Partition/constrain, parameterise or instantiate test data at cypress\fixtures

- Specify test sequences or fully-fledged test behaviours (including control statements and expressions), to parameterise and/or to group them through hooks such as beforeEach, afterEach, Before, After in `commands.js`
- Document the test data (through fixtures), test cases and/or test procedures (through `cypress\integration\features`)

Test Execution Layer of Cypress.io

The test execution layer consists of tool support for the following:

- Executing test cases automatically
- Logging the test case executions
- Reporting the test results

All these three steps are performed by Cypress test runner when getting executed through the command prompt 'npx cypress open'. Alternatively, it can be possible to run the tests through 'Mocha Awesome' as well as 'Mocha Allure Reports'.

The test execution layer of Cypress.io consists of components that provide the following capabilities:

- Set up and tear down test suites (i.e., set of test cases including test data) through configurations such as `cypress.json`, `commands.js` and `index.js`
- Configure and parameterise the test setup using fixtures-based test data
- Interpret both test data and test cases and transform them into executable scripts through spec files in integration folder

- Instrument the test system and/or the SUT for (filtered) logging of test execution and for fault injection through XHR
- Analyse the SUT responses during test execution to steer subsequent test runs with a default wait time of four seconds
- Validate the SUT responses (comparison of expected and actual results) for automated test case execution results with the help of assertions
- Control the automated test execution in time since the tests run inside Cypress test runner that controls browser (instead of other automation test tools that run the browser tests through browser drivers; hence, the control depends on browser drivers)

What Cypress Won't Do?

Set up and tear down the SUT for test execution: Application code can be maintained in the same root of Cypress scripts, but the application has to be launched prior (independent to Cypress) in order to run the Cypress tests on top of it.

Test Adaptation Layer of Cypress.io

The test adaptation layer consists of tool support for the following:

- Controlling the test harness through collection of stubs to mimic API responses and help verifying UI messages and events
- Interacting with the SUT in a controlled browser inside Cypress test runner
- Monitoring the SUT throughout the tests to avoid flakiness
- Simulating or emulating the SUT environment with the help of XHR interceptions of API responses such as error message verification through API

The test adaptation layer provides the following functionality:

■ Mediating between the technology-neutral test definitions and the specific technology requirements of the SUT and the test devices: Cypress.io tests are written in JavaScript-based nodejs bindings and applications need not be written in JavaScript alone. Even if the SUT consists of various technologies and programming languages, it is still possible to test through Cypress.io tests as long as the automated tests are written in JavaScript.

■ Applying different technology-specific adaptors to interact with the SUT: When APIs are not constructed and GUI has to perform or react to an API error response to display such error message on GUI screen, it is possible to script XHR libraries as adaptors to display such error messages, thus verifying GUI for the message display is possible.

■ Distributing the test execution across multiple test devices/test interfaces or executing tests locally: Even though not much options are available to run parallel across devices using local Cypress test runner, integration cloud solutions such as BrowserStack help in running across 2000+ types of browsers, operating systems and device combinations.

■ Default browser support: Cypress.io version 4 onwards supports Google Chrome, Canary, Firefox, Microsoft Edge and Electron.

What is Not Possible with Cypress.io to Match the Needs of Test Adaptation Layers?

Browsers such as Internet Explorer 7, 8, 9 or 10 cannot be used with Cypress.io since Microsoft Edge is the only option in the list of Microsoft browsers, which supports Cypress version 4 onwards. There may be future versions of Cypress support diversified browsers, but no such options of support would be available for browsers such as Opera, Internet Explorer, Netscape Navigator.

Still, some of the users use Internet Explorer to read along with screen readers based on the support of assistive technologies such as JAWS Screen Reader. But, there is no option to test your web applications with the help of Cypress in those older versions.

Chapter 16

Cypress-based API Testing

But, the real challenge depends on the readiness of those API servers to imitate the mechanism of actual API responses when there is no server setup available.

SOAP and REST are most common APIs used for application development and REST contains useful HTTP verbs such as POST, GET, PUT, PATCH and DELETE. GET and POST are the first set of verbs used while verifying the application requests and responses in REST API based on the architecture of the application.

Mocks and Stubs

Any outgoing dependencies such as headers, request body of POST messages can be scripted and known as mocks. Similarly, any incoming dependencies such as response URLs, response body can be scripted to verify the expected outcome and this scripting of API responses is known as stub.

Cypress supports XHR interception and performs body assertion and request URL assertions.

XHR or **XMLH**ttp**R**equest is an application programming interface in the form of an object whose methods transfer data/content between a web browser (during the test) and a web server (for the API testing verifications). The object is provided by the browser's JavaScript environment. Page refresh and calling API request from exclusive portal are not required and XHR capability of cypressautomatically enables the web page to update part of the page itself with disrupting user actions. When user performs a button click and expects to verify an error message, instead of refreshing the page for the API response, it communicates to the web server and loads the error message as per the contract specification.

Let us take an example to understand this from repository: https://github.com/narayananpalani/cypress-api-test-techniques

Application source code in index.html:

```
<!DOCTYPE html>
<html lang="en">
  <head>
    <meta charset="UTF-8" />
    <title>Cypress TDD Tests</title>
  </head>
  <body>
    <main>
      <form>
        <div>
          <label for="name">Name</label>
          <input type="name" required
name="name" id="name" />
        </div>
        <div>
          <label for="email">Email</label>
          <input type="email" required
name="email" id="email" />
        </div>
        <div>
          <label for="message">Your message</
label>
```

```
            <textarea id="message" name="message"
required></textarea>
        </div>
        <div>
            <button type="submit">SEND</button>
        </div>
      </form>
    </main>
  </body>
  <script src="form.js"></script>
</html>
```

Graphical user interface. Check Figure 16.1:
Stubbing through `form.js`.:

```
const form = document.forms[0];

form.addEventListener("submit", event => {
  event.preventDefault();
  new FormData(form);
});

document.addEventListener("formdata", event => {
  const body = Object.fromEntries(event.
formData.entries());
  const jsonBody = JSON.stringify(body);
  const request = new XMLHttpRequest();
```

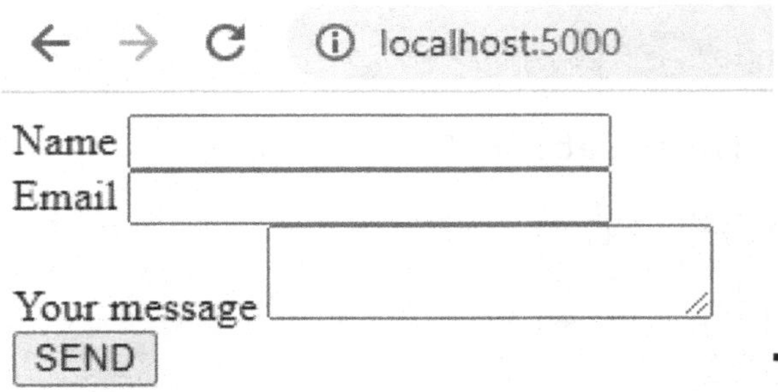

Figure 16.1   Graphical User Interface (GUI)

```
    request.open("POST", "https://jsonplaceholder.
typicode.com/users/");
    request.send(jsonBody);
        // get the response
        request.onload = function() {
            const jsonResponse = JSON.parse(this.
response);
            document.body.innerHTML += 'Response from
the server: ${jsonResponse.status}';
        };
});
```

Commands.js:

```
beforeEach(() => {
    // root-level hook
    // runs before every test
    cy.log('Tests Started');
    cy.visit("/");
    cy.get("form");
  });

  afterEach(() => {
    // runs after each test in the block
    cy.get("form").submit();
    cy.contains("Form saved!");
  });
```

Index.js:

```
import './commands'
```

Spec file at cypress\integration\form.spec.js:

```
describe("Form test", () => {

    it("Can fill the form", () => {


        cy.get('input[name="name"]')
```

```
          .type("Narayanan Palani")
          .should("have.value", "Narayanan
Palani");

          cy.get('input[name="email"]')
          .type("np@dev.dev")
          .should("have.value", "np@dev.dev");

          cy.get("textarea")
          .type("Mind you if I ask some silly
question?")
          .should("have.value", "Mind you if I ask
some silly question?");

          cy.server();
          cy.route({
             url: "/users/**",
             method: "POST",
             response: { status: "Form saved!",
code: 201 }
          });
       });
});
```

Step definition:

```
          cy.server();
          cy.route({
             url: "/users/**",
             method: "POST",
             response: { status: "Form saved!",
code: 201 }
          });
```

Chapter 17

BrowserStack-based Cypress Test Execution

2000+ browsers, operating systems and device combinations are supported by BrowserStack, which can be referred to at https://www.browserstack.com/list-of-browsers-and-platforms/ automate.

How To Test Your Cypress.io Scripts in BrowserStack?

Create your Cypress.io test repository ready with automated tests and run them locally to make sure that the tests get executed as expected and follow the four-step process mentioned in this section to configure and run Cypress tests in BrowserStack cloud.

As pre-requisites, signup and perform registration at https://www.browserstack.com. Capture the username and access key from the tab 'Access Key' on the home page of the

BrowserStack website. This is required in order to perform the test configurations from your automated repository.

1. Installation in repository:
   Navigate to the terminal of your code repository of Cypress.io automated tests and perform installation by

```
npm install -g browserstack-cypress-cli
```

When BrowserStack is installed, the respective code version gets updated into package.json; This means BrowserStack can interact with configuration files to run your tests virtually in the BrowserStack cloud after this installation.

2. Creation of Json file of BrowserStack through browserstack-cypress init:
   Once BrowserStack has been installed, there needs to be a configuration file for BrowserStack within your code repository. So, the cloud services can translate the configurations from the file to understand the path of the tests and respective browser combinations to execute the tests.

   This configuration file can be created by the command,

```
browserstack-cypress init
```

New file named browserstack.json gets created at the root level after this command gets executed.

3. Updation of the browserstack.json using standard configurations:
   Find the sample configuration provided in the repository cypress-test-techniques in Github:

```
{
    "auth": {
        "username": "XXX",
        "access_key": "XXX"
    },
```

```
    "browsers": [
        {
            "browser": "chrome",
            "os": "Windows 10",
            "versions": [
                "78",
                "77"
            ]
        }
    ],
    "run_settings": {
        "cypress_proj_dir": "./",
        "project_name":
"cypress-test-techniques",
        "build_name": "silver-1525",
        "parallels": "5",
        "npm_dependencies": {
            "mem": "6.1.0",
            "minimist": "1.2.5",
            "mochawesome-report-generator":
"4.1.0",
            "npm-run-all": "4.1.2",
            "serve": "11.3.2",
            "through": "2.3.8",
            "@bahmutov/print-env": "1.2.0",
            "@typescript-eslint/eslint-
plugin": "2.24.0",
            "@typescript-eslint/parser":
"2.24.0",
            "allure-commandline": "2.0.0",
            "colon-names": "1.0.0",
            "cypress": "4.11.0",
            "cypress-axe": "0.8.1",
            "cypress-cucumber-preprocessor":
"1.11.0",
            "cypress-file-upload": "4.0.6",
            "cypress-image-snapshot": "3.1.1",
            "cypress-plugin-retries": "1.2.0",
            "cypress-plugin-tab": "1.0.5",
            "cypress-visual-regression":
"1.4.0",
```

```
                    "cypress-xpath": "1.3.0",
                    "eslint": "5.16.0",
                    "eslint-plugin-cypress": "2.8.1",
                    "eslint-plugin-cypress-dev":
"2.1.0",
                    "eslint-plugin-mocha": "5.3.0",
                    "eslint-plugin-vue": "6.2.2",
                    "mocha": "5.2.0",
                    "mocha-allure-reporter": "1.4.0",
                    "mocha-gherkin": "0.2.0",
                    "mochawesome": "6.1.1",
                    "mochawesome-merge": "2.1.0",
                    "start-server-and-test":
"1.10.6",
                    "stop-build": "1.1.0",
                    "stop-only": "3.1.0",
                    "typescript": "3.7.4",
                    "yaml-lint": "1.2.4"
            }
        },
        "connection_settings": {
            "local": false,
            "local_identifier": null
        },
        "disable_usage_reporting": false
}
```

There are more examples available at https://www.browserstack.com/docs/automate/cypress.

Auth Details Sourcing from BrowserStack Website

After signing up in Browserstack website, access key can be taken along with the username from Access Key tab of home page and that has to be provided here:

```
{
    "auth": {
    "username": "XXX",
    "access_key": "XXX"
    },
```

Browser Combinations

In the example given above, I wanted my tests to get executed in a Windows 10 platform with Google Chrome 77 and 78 versions in two separate groups of tests. Similarly, I can increase this to multiple browser combinations based on the scope of browsers to get tested. Alternatively, I can try changing the platform from Windows to Mac OS as well.

In another example, if two different browsers (Chrome and Firefox) need to get tested in separate operating systems such as Windows and MacOS version OS X Mojave, these configurationscan be configured such as below:

```
"browsers": [
    {
        "browser": "chrome",
        "os": "Windows 10",
        "versions": [
            "78",
            "77"
        ]
    },
    {
        "browser": "firefox",
        "os": "OS X Mojave",
        "versions": [
            "66",
            "65"
        ]
    }
],
```

Run Settings

Within "run_settings", project-related configuration needs to be provided for the tool to understand how to source the automated test code.

"cypress_proj_dir": "./"

Every Cypress.io-based automated test repository is provided with `cypress.json` configuration at the root level. This has to be configured inside "cypress_proj_dir" such as. /; hence, it helps the cloud tool in navigating inside json file and taking the project details.

"project_name": "cypress-test-techniques"

Give the project name with your repository name, which should be meaningful and understandable in order to compare the history of tests later in the test history.

"build_name": "silver-1525"

It is advisable to provide the build number of source code of Cypress.io tests within "build_name"; hence, this test can easily be located in BrowserStack website.

"parallels": "5"

Performing parallel tests is the key attribute to find defects when multiple user interactions go through the application under test. This is possible when parallels is updated part of `browserstack.json`.

"npm_dependencies"

The entire set of tools used within the automation repository needs to be sourced from `package.json` and provide them within the section 'npm_dependencies' to help BrowserStack to run tests on the cloud.

"connection_settings"

Cypress.io is the most helpful tool if implemented along with application development; hence, the source code of the application is built local. In such a situation, it is not a feasible approach to load the source code into BrowserStack and run the tests virtually there. Instead, BrowserStack tests can run local where source code is deployed and launched in order to get it tested.

If the application URL is already available and deployed with public site access, it can be configured to test with "local": false.

"disable_usage_reporting"

Every command-line argument is used, system details and errors are captured by BrowserStack when "disable_usage_reporting" has been marked as false, which is the default configuration. But, this can be marked true in order to protect the data and usage of the teams based on the needs.

4. Run the tests in BrowserStack:
Once `browserstack.json` has been configured, it is easy to run the Cypress tests by executing the command in the terminal such as

```
browserstack-cypress run
```

Alternative option to disable the usage reporting while running the tests is

```
browserstack-cypress run
-disable-usage-reporting
```

All these configurations are provided in the sample Github repository and it can be tried from https://github.com/narayananpalani/cypress-test-techniques.

Once tests are executed from repository, live status of the test execution and results are available from BrowserStack website with the clear differentiation using build name and project name.

Running The Tests Local:

Perform BrowserStack installation by

```
npm install browserstacklocal
```

Once installed, update the configuration such as

```
{
    "auth": {
        "username": "naru3",
        "access_key": "BCC6eBHFEuPq7vpCMyqa"
    },
    "browsers": [
        {
            "browser": "chrome",
            "os": "Windows 10",
            "versions": [
                "78"
            ]
        }
    ],
    "run_settings": {
        "cypress_proj_dir": "./",
        "project_name":
"cypress-api-test-techniques",
        "build_name": "bronze-1127",
        "parallels": "3",
        "npm_dependencies": {
        }
    },
    "connection_settings": {
        "local": true,
        "local_identifier": "apiTests1"
    },
    "disable_usage_reporting": true
}
```

So, marking "local": true helps to run the tests within the same local of source code and more configurations are available from the website: https://www.browserstack.com/docs/automate/cypress/local-testing

Try running the local tests by cloning the sample repository from: https://github.com/narayananpalani/cypress-api-test-techniques

Test Strategy for Running Device Compatibility Tests Using BrowserStack

Usually, application development team may not be provided with multiple operating systems and different devices to test the application behaviour across browser types. Thus, testing Cypress.io verifications using BrowserStack is one of the wonderful option to identify defects with different browser versions. Installing different browser versions of Google Chrome within various laptops and trying the application behaviour is simply not a viable option. Instead, configuring them in `browserstack.json` and running them in respective browser version virtually gives a hint of application stability on those version combinations. In my experience, dropdowns and images behave differently when verified in browsers such as Microsoft Edge and older versions of Firefox. Checkboxes and pre-populated texts within text boxes are also potential areas to check when different browsers are used. Taking user survey with the various browser types they use needs to be considered while selecting the configurations in `browserstack.json`.

Chapter 18

Capture/Playback Approach of Test Automation

There are various modern Google Chrome Extensions available to capture the user interactions and convert them to Cypress.io scripts automatically!

Fd Cypress Recorder

This recorder can be installed from Google Chrome Extensions Link, https://chrome.google.com/webstore/detail/ fd-cypress-recorder/amleackadkomdccpbfginhnecfhhognj?hl =en

Once installed, record button needs to be clicked to start performing user interactions and continue until the required step to click on Stop button of this extension at the end. Cypress scripts get ready to use it in the framework from there on. This recorder is more appropriate for BDD-based step definitions since it creates the scripts in step definition formats.

There are few more recording Google Chrome Extensions, which can be used to record every step towards line by line Cypress scripts.

Cypress Scenario Recorder

This recorder can be installed from Google Chrome Extensions Link, https://chrome.google.com/webstore/detail/cypress-scenario-recorder/fmpgoobcionmfneadjapdabmjfkmfekb/related?hl=en

Cypress Recorder

This recorder can be installed from Google Chrome Extensions Link, https://chrome.google.com/webstore/detail/cypress-recorder/glcapdcacdfkokcmicllhcjigeodacab

Even though these three recorders are helpful in creating Cypress scripts, no solution is found until 2020 to playback those recorded scripts and let us hope some innovative Chrome Extensions to get created to perform playback of those recorded scripts in near future.

Chapter 19

Test Applications with Slow Speed Using Cypress.io and URL Throttler

When a same page loads with extended delays due to network traffic and users try to hit buttons several times either by keyboard or by mouse clicks, there are possibilities of defects, which may not be realised unless tested with such odd combinations.

In fact, this is the most common scenario to try and the most common miss by majority of the QAs in the world.

Let me take a real-time situation to explain this possibility. I had to travel to work on London tube trains and every time, I had less time to book tickets for movies online or book the flight tickets while travelling on a high-speed train with low mobile connectivity. So, I got the page loaded and started booking with customer details on the flight information, and by the time I reached the flight reservation final button, I crossed several underground stations in which the mobile network was not possible. So, the page needs to continue the active session and at the same time, it should let me book the ticket even in such odd situation of intermittent network connectivity. If you think it is not a valid scenario to get it tested, it is a mistaken judgement. Most of the working professionals travel to work or travel while accessing some of the essential websites.

How can such slowness of network connectivity be reproduced in Cypress tests?

URL Throttler is a Google Chrome Extension, which can cause delays while performing tests using Cypress.io.

If you install or add this extension to your Google Chrome browser on laptop, it will not be visible while running the tests from Cypress Test Runner to launch Google Chrome. Since Chrome launched from Cypress is controlled by Cypress runner itself, the extension has to be added when Chrome browser is launched through Cypress test runner.

Open a new tab when Cypress test runner has launched Google Chrome and enter the URL of URL Throttler to add it to Chrome.

Google Chrome Extension can be installed by: https://chrome.google.com/webstore/detail/url-throttler/ kpkeghonflnkockcnaegmphgdldfnden

When URL Throttler is added to the Chrome of Cypress as shown in Figure 19.1, then click on 'Enabled' of URL Throttle and provide the URL you want to delay and delay time in milliseconds.

Figure 19.1 URL Throttler installed within Google Chrome of Cypress.io (display during the chrome launching time of test execution)

If you re-run your tests with Cypress test runner and Chrome as browser, you can see the same website loaded with time delay and you can see some of the tests passed earlier in Cypress may fail when the page is loaded with delayed time and you need to investigate on to find the nature of defect such as Cypress script failure or the application failure while dealing with the page load time.

Chapter 20

DAST with Cypress.io and BurpSuite

In this section, we are going to see how Cypress tests can help performing BurpSuite Vulnerability Scan as part of Dynamic Application Security Testing (DAST).

When web applications are getting developed, scanning a few numbers of pages is easy, but it will be a challenge if there are hundreds of pages getting developed. Automation testing is primarily helpful to test when huge number of pages are getting built. Now, the primary trick is to use the same automated tests built in Cypress to reuse for DAST.

Step 1:
Every DAST Security Scanner such as BurpSuite provides an option to configure proxy. In Burpsuite, it can be configured at 'Proxy' tab to choose 'Options' section and click 'Add' to enter 'localhost:8080' as an example.
Step 2:
Launch Cypress Tests through Mozilla Firefox and navigate to Network Settings of Firefox. Select 'Manual Proxy Configuraiton' and enter HTTP Proxy as 127.0.0.1 or localhost; enter port as 8080.

This configuration can be done for other browsers and instructions are available at https://portswigger.net/support/configuring-your-browser-to-work-with-burp.

Step 3:

Rerun the Cypress.io tests from Mozilla Firefox when BurpSuite is launched in the background.

Step 4:

Complete tests from Cypress.io. Navigate to BurpSuite, which is running in the background during Cypress tests and right click on the relevant path of the web domain or URL and click Crawl optionto perform 'Crawl' on those websites to find security vulnerabilities.

Chapter 21

Click Function Using Cypress.io

What every tutorial tries to teach is just one bit about `cy.click()`, but in fact, this is not good enough for a beginner who tries to understand how to get it implemented by stages. Even if you are a mid-level experienced test lead and trying to implement BDD into Cypress.io, its easy only when you are aware of the steps involved in getting the functions called in sequential order.

Step 1: Introduce a feature file at `cypress\integration\features\*.feature folder level`

```
Feature: Login Test on ABC website

Scenario: Check valid signIn attempt with valid
user and password credentials
        Given I open ABC homepage
        When I SignIn as user
        Then the user name should be displayed
```

Once feature file is written, the next step is to write step definitions to associate each line of feature file with the corresponding Cypress code. The Gherkin format of BDD code given above is nothing but a basic skeleton of user scenarios and the actual code formulating the automation instructions is followed only when a definition written for those lines is mentioned above.

Step 2: Write step definitions at `cypress\support\` `step _ definitions\*.js folder level`

```
import { loginPage } from '../../pageobjects/
Login_PageObjects'
When('I SignIn as user', () => {
  loginOrangehrmPage.signIn()
})
```

The import line is to link the functions written for signIn to the corresponding step definition described above. Similarly, the code within the lines of 'when' and the template used after it (inside step definitions) are the standard format used;.

Step 3: Write functions within page objects at `cypress\` `pageobjects\Login _ PageObjects.js folder` `level`

Import the commands from `commands.js` in order to use some nice plugins such as cypress-xpath

```
import { terminalLog } from '../support/
commands.js'
```

Provide objects or data locators of the web page used to detect particular section of the web page to perform action:

```
const inputUserName = '//input[@
id=\'txtUsername\']'
const inputUserPassword = '#txtPassword'
const loginButtonSubmit = '//*[@
id=\'btnLogin\']'
const label_Welcome = '//*[@id=\'welcome\']'
```

Write a small export function to provide inputs to perform actions and events on those objects provided as constants in the page object file:

```
export const loginPage = {
  launchPage () {
    cy.visit('/')
          .injectAxe()
  },
  enterUsername (args) {
    cy.xpath(inputUserName)
          .click()
          .clear()
          .type(args)
  },
  enterPassword (args) {
    cy.get(inputUserPassword)
          .click()
          .clear()
          .type(args)
  },
  clickSubmit () {
    cy.xpath(loginButtonSubmit)
          .click()
  },
  signIn () {
    cy.fixture('testdata').then((data) => {
      this.enterUsername(data.username)
      this.enterPassword(data.password)
      this.clickSubmit()
      cy.wait(2000)
    })
  }
}
```

Let us understand the click functionality underneath each function written here.

enterUsername taking the data as argument and passing on to the type step(to enter the data on text box);If there are cookies captured for particular websites or pre-populated data available on a particular text box, it is recommended to click and clear them before typing the expected text. Hence, I followed an approach to click on the text box, clear the contents whatever pre-populated and type finally with the args passed on from the function which is args:

```
enterUsername (args) {
  cy.xpath(inputUserName)
        .click()
        .clear()
        .type(args)
},
```

Similar approach is followed by parsing the data such as password through args to enterPassword function and getting the object through get. If you carefully notice, I have used `cy.xpath` for username and `cy.get` for password. This is because I want to show the difference between calling the xpath and css locators. Since password field locator is captured as '#txtPassword', it is appropriate to call this as `cy.get` in order to recognise the locator. Similar to the username field, I have clicked on the text box, cleared it and entered password through .type:

```
enterPassword (args) {
  cy.get(inputUserPassword)
        .click()
        .clear()
        .type(args)
```

After entering username and password, I want to click on submit button. Hence, another function is written below to perform click action on top of the submit button through the xpath locator '//*[@id=\'welcome\']':

```
clickSubmit () {
  cy.xpath(loginButtonSubmit)
```

```
            .click()
    },
```

Now, all small functions are written to describe each event around the objects such as username, password and submit button, but it has to be called within a function in order to link it to step definition:

```
signIn () {
    cy.fixture('testdata').then((data) => {
        this.enterUsername(data.username)
        this.enterPassword(data.password)
        this.clickSubmit()
        cy.wait(2000)
    })
}
```

Chapter 22

Adjusting Default Timeouts or Wait Times in Cypress.json

Unlike other test automation frameworks, Cypress comes with a default command timeout of four seconds (or 4000 milliseconds). It means the tool waits for the object to appear within four seconds in order to perform the commands and there is no need to write specific wait code in the scripts for it. But, if this needs to be changed to 60 seconds, it can be altered in Cypress.json file by adding the configuration as below:

```
{
    "defaultCommandTimeout": 60000
}
```

Similarly, some of the test environments are usually slow in launching the websites first time. It can be controlled with the below timeout configuration (which is waiting for two minutes to load the page):

```
{
    "pageLoadTimeout": 120000
}
```

Commands such as *cy.visit()*, *cy.go()*, *cy.reload()* are used in order to load the web pages and they are controlled by the pageLoadTimeout given above.

If the websites are built with XHR API stubs, it is appropriate to configure those timeouts when there are possibilities of delays while getting the responses from those stubs written for the Cypress frameworks. In this example, scripts are waiting up to 30 seconds to get an XHR response every time.

```
{
  "responseTimeout": 30000
}
```

This response timeout is applicable when commands such as *cy.request()*, *cy.wait()*, *cy.fixture()*, *cy.getCookie()*, *cy.getCookies()*, *cy.setCookie()*, *cy.clearCookie()*, *cy.clearCookies()*, and *cy.screenshot()* are used as per Cypress documentation.

Similar to the response timeout above, if there are validations around API requests (header, body) and wait through `cy.wait()`, it can be controlled with similar configuration as well:

```
{
  "requestTimeout": 30000
}
```

Finally, execTimeout (for the usage of *cy.exec()*) and taskTimeout (for the usage of *cy.task()*) are less common when using the commands in the Cypress framework. But, they are also clearly defined by Cypress and can be controlled through the custom configurations in `cypress.json` file.

After using necessary timeouts configurations, my `cypress.json` looks like below:

```
{
  "projectId": "j5qpgn",
  "baseUrl": "https://opensource-demo.
orangehrmlive.com",
```

```
"waitForAnimations": true,
"animationDistanceThreshold": 50,
"pageLoadTimeout": 120000,
"defaultCommandTimeout": 60000,
"requestTimeout": 30000,
"chromeWebSecurity": false,
"watchForFileChanges": false,
"trashAssetsBeforeRuns": true,
 "reporter": "mochawesome",
  "reporterOptions": {
   "overwrite": false
  }

}
```

Chapter 23

Double Click Function Using Cypress.io

An article comprising its details can be referred to at https://baymard.com/blog/users-double-click-online.

Such user actions such as double click can be verified with the help of Cypress.io within a few seconds.

Step 1: Introduce a feature file at `cypress\integration\features\*.feature` folder level:

```
Feature: Purchase products on ABC website
Scenario: Check Product Purchase feature with
double click user behaviour
        Given I login to ABC website
        When I select a product with one
quantity using mouse double click
        Then the product should be ordered with
one quantity successfully
```

Once feature file is written, the next step is to imitate the behaviour of mouse clicks in step definitions. It is advisable to write those double clicks within a function and call it from step definition.

Step 2: Write step definitions at `cypress\support\`
`step _ definitions\*.js folder level`:

```
import { ShoppingPage } from '../../
pageobjects/Purchase_PageObjects'
When(' I select a product with one quantity
using mouse double click', () => {
  ShoppingPage.DoubleClickPurchase()
})
```

DoubleClickPurchase is a function called from step definition in which the actual dblclick action is written.

Step 3: Write functions within page objects at `cypress\`
`pageobjects\Purchase _ PageObjects.js folder`
`level.`
Import the commands from commands.js in order to use some nice plugins such as cypress-xpath:

```
import { terminalLog } from '../support/
commands.js'
```

Declare the xpath locator of buy button next to the target product as constant:

```
const ProductItem2_Buy= '//*[@id=\'ID2343\']'
```

Now, write a small function that identifies this xpath and perform double click using .dblclick():

```
DoubleClickPurchase () {
  cy.xpath(ProductItem2_Buy)
        .dblclick()
},
```

In my experience, verifying the user behaviour in front-end is limited since a user just performs double click and expects to see a success message or email confirmation, whereas the quantity ordered has to be verified with the help of microservices and back-end systems confirmation. So, it may not be just one test to perform end-to-end to get the entire verification done in a few seconds. But, getting this test extended to those downstream systems (purchase order systems) will help in verifying the quantity being ordered and delivered to the users.

Types of Defects Expected in Double Click User Behaviour

Many e-commerce websites show a spinning wheel after a product purchase through 'Buy' button or 'Order Now' button. When a user clicks on the 'Order Now' button, there may be a spinning wheel display for a few milliseconds with greyed out background. But, the button in the background would be active and the user still can navigate with keyboard action to perform click or double click either through mouse or through keyboards. These kind of behaviours need exploratory testing and adding those proven tests with defects to the Cypress test pack will help rerunning those edge case tests as part of regression suite.

What If the Spinning Wheel Disappears Within a Few Milliseconds?

When a user clicks on 'Order Now', a spinning wheel appears for a few milliseconds before displaying success or confirmation message, It is possible to slow it down with the help of Google Chrome Extensions such as URL Throttler. So, the success message is delayed by extending the spinning wheel for some more time. Hence, Cypress tests can perform button clicks or double clicks to re-create the edge cases, which the real-time users may try with slow wifi connectivity.

Chapter 24

Cypress Retry on Failed Tests

Defect: https://github.com/cypress-io/cypress/issues/4694

These kinds of automation tool defects (not the application failure) can be prevented to get clear test results with retry option. Otherwise, test results show some failures in which rerun would pass the same tests, which were failed earlier due to those tool defects.

Cypress.json can be configured as below:

```
{
  "retries": {
  // Configure retries for `cypress run`
  // Default is 2
  "runMode": 1,
  // Configure retries for `cypress open`
  // Default is 0
  "openMode": 1
  }
}
```

I have configured one retry for both Cypress run and Cypress open mode in the example above in order to overcome any tool issues to rerun those failed tests and provide a clean report with no false negatives (failed due to automation tool, but not due to application failure).

In addition to automation tool issues, it is also good to have retries to run those failed tests once again to verify any failure due to application load issues. I have tried many XHR responses with URL Throttler (Google Chrome Extension) to understand how GUI reacts when API responses are delayed. In such cases, it is worth to have retry option as 1 or more in order to get the clear behaviour or pattern of GUI display for those edge case scenarios.

If you don't want to get any retry for your tests when they are failed, it is easy to configure them as 0 in **cypress.json** as below:

```
{
  "retries": 0
}
```

## Chapter 25

Mouse Events Using Cypress.io

Hover over on the objects such as images using
`.trigger('mouseover')`.

When a user scrolls a particular image or link of the
website, it may display a small pop up message or content
related to the particular section of object. This can be imitated
with the help of mouse over command of Cypress.io.

Perform mouse down on links with the help of
`.trigger('mousedown')`.

Mouse down is regularly performed by the users on links,
which show additional content about such links when this action is
performed. So, these trigger events can be performed and Cypress
also produces videos of those interactions for getting them cross-
checked later on (videos are stored at cypress/videos folder).

If you think videos are not required, they can be turned off
at **cypress.json** by setting **"video": false**.

Step 1: Write a feature file with the list of scenarios that
includes mouse interactions:

```
Feature: Home Page Mouse Movement Test on ABC
website
```

Scenario: Right Click on Admin Tab of home page
    Given I open ABC homepage
    When I SignIn as user
    And I click on admin tab of home page
    And I move **mouse down** on admin tab section
    Then the Admin tab should be displayed
Scenario: Touch start on Admin Tab of home page
    Given I open ABC homepage
    When I SignIn as user
    And I click on admin tab of home page
    And I move **touchstart** using mouse on admin tab section
    Then the Admin tab should be displayed

Scenario: Mouseover on Admin Tab Results of home page
    Given I open ABC homepage
    When I SignIn as user
    And I click on admin tab of home page
    And I **mouseover** on first row of results table of admin tab
    And I **mouseover** on second row of results table of admin tab
    Then the Admin tab should be displayed

Scenario: Mouseleave on Admin Tab Results of home page
    Given I open ABC homepage
    When I SignIn as user
    And I click on admin tab of home page
    And I **mouseover** on first row of results table of admin tab
    And I **mouseleave** on first row of results table of admin tab
    Then the Admin tab should be displayed

Scenario: Mouseactions on Dashboard Tab Graph
    Given I open ABC homepage
    When I SignIn as user

```
    When I perform move actions on dashboard
graph
    Then text insights displayed below
dashboard successfully
```

Step 2: Write step definitions to those feature file Gherkin scenarios:

```
When('I move mouse down on admin tab
section', () => {
  abcPage.mousedownAdminTab()
})
When('I move touchstart using mouse on admin
tab section', () => {
  abcPage.touchAdminTab()
})
When('I move mouseover using mouse on admin
tab section', () => {
  abcPage.mouseoverAdminTab()
})
When('I click on first row of results table
of admin tab', () => {
  abcPage.clickAdminResultTableR1C2()
})
When('I mouseover on first row of results
table of admin tab', () => {
  abcPage.mouseOverAdminResultTableR1C2()
})
When('I mouseleave on first row of results
table of admin tab', () => {
  abcPage.mouseleaveAdminResultTableR1C2()
})
When('I mouseover on second row of results
table of admin tab', () => {
  abcPage.mouseOverAdminResultTableR2C2()
})
When('I perform move actions on dashboard
graph', () => {
  abcPage.mousActionsonDashboardGraph()
})
```

Step 3: Write functions for those mouse interactions with the help of Cypress commands.

It is recommended to write the object locators outside functions for better clarity and ease of maintenance. I have provided some sample object locators in this section, which are used in the functions for mouse interactions:

```
const admin_tabselector_Homepage =
'#menu_admin_viewAdminModule'
const admin_resultTableRow1Column2 = '//*[@
id=\'resultTable\']/tbody/tr[1]/td[2]'
const admin_resultTableRow2Column2 = '//*[@
id=\'resultTable\']/tbody/tr[2]/td[2]'
const graph_dashboard = '//*[@
id=\'div_graph_display_emp_distribution\']'
const pieChartLabel1 = '//*[@
id=\'pieLabel1\']/div'
const pieChartLabel2 = '//*[@
id=\'pieLabel2\']/div'
const pieChartLabel3 = '//*[@
id=\'pieLabel3\']/div'
const pieChartLabel4 = '//*[@
id=\'pieLabel4\']/div'
const admin_tabxPath_Homepage = '//*[@
id=\'menu_admin_viewAdminModule\']'
```

Now, write a function for each mouse event with the help of Cypress trigger commands.

```
export const abcPage = {

  mousedownAdminTab () {
    cy.xpath(admin_tabxPath_Homepage)
      .invoke('show').should('be.visible')
      .trigger('mousedown')
  },
  touchAdminTab () {
    cy.xpath(admin_tabxPath_Homepage)
      .invoke('show').should('be.visible')
```

```
      .trigger('touchstart')
  },
  mouseoverAdminTab () {
    cy.xpath(admin_tabxPath_Homepage)
      .invoke('show').should('be.visible')
      .trigger('mouseover')
  },
  mouseOverAdminResultTableR1C2 () {
    cy.xpath(admin_resultTableRow1Column2)
      .invoke('show').should('be.visible')
      .trigger('mouseover')
  },
  mouseleaveAdminResultTableR1C2 () {
    cy.xpath(admin_resultTableRow1Column2)
      .invoke('show').should('be.visible')
      .trigger('mouseleave')
  },
  mouseOverAdminResultTableR2C2 () {
    cy.xpath(admin_resultTableRow2Column2)
      .invoke('show').should('be.visible')
      .trigger('mouseover')
  },
  mousActionsonDashboardGraph () {
    cy.xpath(graph_dashboard)
      .as('graph')
      .trigger('mousedown')
      .trigger('mousemove')
      .trigger('mouseup')
      .trigger('mouseleft', { which: 1, pageX:
600, pageY: 100 })
      .trigger('mouseright', { which: 1, pageX:
600, pageY: 600 })
      .trigger('mouseleave')
  }
}
```

These trigger commands are unique to Cypress and really helpful in reproducing the user behaviour with the help of mouse interactions.

## Chapter 26

Checkboxes Verification Using Cypress.io

But, it is highly advisable to check those boxes only when they are enabled. So, it is worth to cross-check the object to make sure it is not disabled in order to click on it to check it:

```
checkEmployees () {
  cy.xpath(selectAll_pimTab)
      .not('[disabled]')
      .check()
},
```

Once checkbox is selected, it can be verified with the help of `.should` command as below:

```
allEmployeesSelected () {
  cy.xpath(selectAll_pimTab)
      .not('[disabled]')
      .should('be.checked')
},
```

If a checkbox needs to be unchecked, it is advisable to make sure that the checkbox is not disabled and perform `.uncheck` as below:

```
uncheckEmployees () {
  cy.xpath(selectAll_pimTab)
    .not('[disabled]')
    .should('be.checked')
    .uncheck()
},
```

Once a checkbox is unchecked, it can be verified with a small function that consists of `.should` command as below:

```
noEmployeesSelected () {
    cy.xpath(selectAll_pimTab)
      .not('[disabled]')
      .should('not.be.checked')
  }
```

Index

Printed in the United States
By Bookmasters